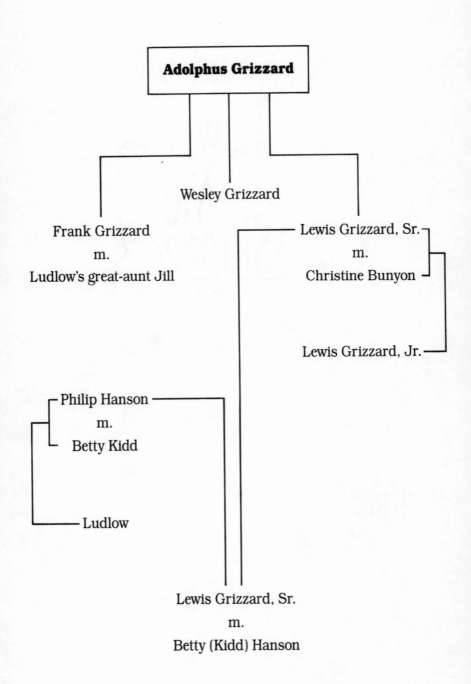

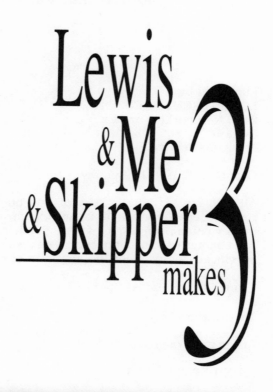

Lewis & Me & Skipper makes 3

makes

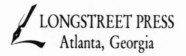

ludlow porch

LONGSTREET PRESS
Atlanta, Georgia

To my friend Bo Whaley, who
understands and loves my
South as much as I do.

Published by
LONGSTREET PRESS, INC.
2150 Newmarket Parkway
Suite 102
Marietta, Georgia 30067

Printed in the United States of America

1st printing, 1991

Library of Congress Catalog Number 91-061937

ISBN 1-56352-009-5

This book was printed by R. R. Donnelley & Sons,
Harrisonburg, Virginia. The text was set in Bookman
by Typo-Repro Service, Inc., Atlanta, Georgia.
Jacket design by Don Bratton.
Jacket photo by Floyd Jillson.
Book design by Jill Dible.

Acknowledgments

Many thanks to all of Skip's
rowdy friends, some who
confessed and some who
didn't; especially to Ron
Jenkins, who is guilty of
everything I have accused him
of and lots more.

INTRODUCTION

Skip Grizzard (you may know him as Lewis) and I would be cousins anyway, since his uncle Frank married my great-aunt Jill. But when his father, Lewis Grizzard, Sr., married my mother, Betty Hanson, we became brothers. The result is that I know everything I ever wanted to know about the Grizzard family—and then some.

What a clan! The remarkable thing about the Grizzard men is that they somehow managed to escape the shadow of Puritanism that has kept so many of us others from learning how to enjoy ourselves. Among the Grizzard men that I have known personally, more glasses have been hoisted, more skirts have been chased, more hearts broken, more antics perpetrated, and more lies told than can possibly be recounted in the pages that follow.

And how I love them! I don't quite understand it, but there's more charm, wit, and just plain fun in a Grizzard fingernail than there is in most states (especially northern ones). They might not always have been the most dependable people in the world, particularly if their money or the sweat of their brow was being counted upon, but if a Grizzard did make the scene, one thing was certain: a good time was at hand.

From his own books and columns, thousands of readers are already familiar with Skip's character, for better or for worse. All I can add is, he came by it honestly.

Frank Grizzard, Esquire

Actually, the first Grizzard to enter my life was not Lewis Grizzard, Sr., but his brother, my uncle Frank Grizzard. He married my great-aunt Jill in about 1945.

I'm not completely sure, but he was either her fourth or fifth husband. In a time when divorce was very, very uncommon in the South, my great-aunt Jill changed husbands like other folks changed their socks.

I was only eleven when they married, but I remember well what the family talk was. Everyone seemed to agree on two things: he was a fine lawyer and he loved to drink.

Uncle Frank was a binge drinker. He would stay completely sober and productive for many months. Then he would take one drink, and that one drink would send his thirst into overdrive. He would stay with it until he was just too drunk or too sick to continue. Sometimes his trips into the bottle lasted for a week, and he would wind up hundreds of miles from where he took his first drink. He would then call Aunt Jill, and she would travel wherever he was to bring him home.

He would always be sick coming home. I don't mean just sick. It seemed to me that his life was hanging by a thread. He would moan and groan, and I'm sure he set all kinds of interstate vomiting records.

He called Aunt Jill "Miss Willie," and between moans he would beg both God and Aunt Jill to help.

"Dear Gawd," he would moan in his rich Southern accent, "if You will let me get better, I'll never take another drink of that filthy liquid. Please, Gawd, spare your servant's life. . . . Miss Willie, you got to get me a drink. Can't you see I'm dying?"

I don't know what the Lord did for him, but Aunt Jill said, "Now Frankie, honey, you know you can't have any whiskey. Here . . . drink this sauerkraut juice. You'll feel better." Somehow she had the idea that sauerkraut juice was just what Uncle Frank needed to return from the dead.

I don't know if it was the Lord, Aunt Jill, or the sauerkraut juice, but in about a week he would be back at work, apparently none the worse for wear.

Uncle Frank was a very handsome man. He was about five feet, ten inches tall, weighed about 260, and had a full head of gray hair. He dressed like a million dollars. I don't remember ever seeing him when he wasn't wearing a shirt and tie.

He had a quick wit and a loving way; it was impossible to be around for any length of time without falling under the spell of his charm. If he had an enemy on earth, I don't know who it was.

He was doing free legal work for poor people long before it was fashionable. One Sunday at the little church he attended in Red Oak, Georgia, he noticed that the young preacher was wearing a threadbare suit. The very next day he took him to his clothing store and bought him two suits. No one ever knew about this gift until the preacher told the story while conducting Uncle Frank's funeral.

But one of the things I remember most about Uncle Frank was the way he handled Aunt Jill. She talked like a Gatling gun and could go several minutes without taking a breath, jumping from one subject to another without the slightest continuity. When he could stand the verbal torrent no longer, Uncle Frank would say, "Miss Willie, in the name of Gawd, would you just hush for five minutes?"

Aunt Jill would laugh and say, "Oh, Frankie! You're just awful."

Uncle Frank tried hard to be tolerant of Aunt Jill's many flights into strangeness. He loved her greatly and overlooked what he was able to overlook.

One night when I was having dinner with them, I was sitting in the den with Uncle Frank while Aunt Jill was cooking dinner. We had a good view of the kitchen from our chairs, and we happened to see Aunt Jill knock a super-large jar of instant coffee off the counter. It made a terrific crash and shattered into a billion pieces.

We kept watching as she got a tea strainer from the cupboard and attempted to strain the broken glass from the coffee.

About ten minutes later there was another ear-jarring crash. This time she had broken a huge jar of peanut butter. While she was turning in circles trying to decide what to do, Uncle Frank looked at me over his glasses and said in his soft drawl, "Ludlow, if she tries to strain that peanut butter, I'm leavin'."

Uncle Frank was a very logical man. If he had any superstitions at all, I never heard him mention them. Aunt Jill, on the other hand, made it a policy to believe in all, absolutely all, superstitions. She believed in all forms of fortune-telling, from reading Tarot cards to reading tea leaves. She often said, seriously, that her life was ruled by the stars. She believed that if you wanted to bring someone bad luck, you put cemetery dirt on their property. If she burned her hand, she would whisper to it in order to "talk the fire out." She believed in black magic, white magic, voodoo, and having the bumps on her head read.

Uncle Frank never said so, but it was obvious that he thought she was about a half-bubble out of plumb.

We were playing cards at his house one night, while a little Chihuahua dog yipped around our feet.

"What does a dog like that cost?" I asked.

"About fifty dollars," Aunt Jill answered.

I saw a good chance to rib Uncle Frank and said, "I never thought I would live to see the day Frank Grizzard would pay fifty dollars for a dog you could fit in your pocket."

Uncle Frank said, "That ain't none of my dog. Your Aunt Jill bought him."

"Well, Frankie," Aunt Jill shot back, "if that dog will cure little Helen's asthma, it's worth every dime I paid for it."

Uncle Frank looked over his glasses and inquired, "Cure asthma, will it?"

"Everybody knows that a Chihuahua will cure asthma," Aunt Jill declared.

Uncle Frank slowly laid his cards on the table and spoke to me as if Aunt Jill were not in the room. "Ludlow," he said, "every year this great country sends millions of dollars to Africa to educate the heathen, and we have this vast ignorance right here in our own midst."

The Great Depression hit the legal profession hard. It was so tough to make a living practicing law that many attorneys became barbers, butchers, truck drivers, or anything else to keep the wolf away from the door.

Uncle Frank decided to stick it out and try to stay with his practice until, as he said, "things picked up." He was forced to fire his secretary and sell most of his office fixtures just to keep the rent paid.

He hadn't collected a fee in months, and one day as he was sitting in his office with fifteen cents in his pocket, a man walked in and said, "I'm looking for Frank Grizzard."

"Sir," Uncle Frank replied, "you have the honor of addressing Frank Grizzard."

"I have been told," the man explained, "that you are the finest criminal lawyer south of Richmond, Virginia."

"Your information is absolutely correct, sir," Uncle Frank assured him. "How may I serve you?"

The man answered that he had been charged with murder and was out on bond. "I want to know how much you will charge to defend me."

"I routinely get five thousand dollars for a murder case," Uncle Frank informed him. "Do you have five thousand dollars, sir?"

The man dropped his head and said, "I only have one hundred and fifty dollars."

"Well, give it here," Uncle Frank allowed. "Never let it be said that Frank Grizzard would stoop to quibble."

Later on, one of the great joys of my life was going to court to watch Uncle Frank try a case. I was a young law student and was trying to learn everything I could about the law, in class and out.

He called me one day and said he was trying a rape case in Lawrenceville and that I should come up, watch, and take some notes. I told him to expect me, but I ran late and didn't arrive until Uncle Frank was half-way through his closing argument.

Uncle Frank was defending the alleged rapist, a soldier, and of course his job was to raise doubts as to the integrity of the alleged victim. I have to say he was a master in front of a jury. As I arrived, he was saying, " . . . and furthermore, ladies and gentlemen of the jury, while this brave American boy was defending you and me against the yellow menace on the bald, frozen hills of Korea"— at this point he whirled and pointed at the woman—"that harlot yonder was seen at Shorty's Beer Joint dancing on a table and eatin' raw weenies."

I had to leave the courtroom or bust out laughing. I never found out what her eating raw weenies had to do with the case. If I knew, the story would probably not strike me so funny.

On another occasion Uncle Frank was defending a man accused of bootlegging. One look at this old boy and you'd believe he was guilty not only of making liquor but, given half a chance, of breaking every law on the Georgia statute books.

Throughout the entire trial, a lady and two small children sat on the very first row of the courtroom, and the woman spent most of the time softly sobbing into a handkerchief. It was such a sad scene that nobody in the room could keep his eyes off her.

When it was time for the closing argument, Uncle Frank was as brilliant as ever. He paced up and down in front of the jury box and in that deep wonderful voice said, "Ladies and gentlemen of the jury, we are prepared to concede that from time to time my client did make and sell just enough corn liquor to keep body and soul together. There are still, thank God, folks in this grand old country who believe that it is better to bend a silly law than to have his family on the public dole or standin' in a welfare line takin' taxpayers' money. Thank God, ladies and gentlemen, that there are still some men around who think their family should be supported by them and not by the government. Thank God, ladies and gentlemen, for the spirit of free enterprise that beats in my client's chest. Make a little liquor? Yes! Go on welfare? Never!"

It was at this point that I fully expected the jury to break into applause, and they might as well have. After less than an hour's deliberation, they found the bootlegger innocent.

When Uncle Frank and I were walking to the car, I mentioned how pitiful the bootlegger's wife and children had looked.

"Wife? What wife?" asked Uncle Frank.

"The lady sitting on the front row was not his wife?"

"Nawww," drawled Uncle Frank. "He ain't never been married. That was a lady I gave fifty dollars to sit on the front row and squall."

Uncle Frank died in 1958. He brought a great deal of laughter into my life and I still miss him. I am convinced that the angels must have rejoiced when they saw my Uncle Frank coming.

Skip's Daddy Was a Pistol

Uncle Frank's brother, Lewis Grizzard, Sr., was one of the people in my life that I loved and admired with all my heart. I'm sure as you read on, you'll sometimes wonder why. I wonder myself. He has been dead for many years now, but he was so full of life that to this day I still can't believe he's gone. Even after all these years, whenever the phone rings, I hope for an instant it will be his voice I hear on the line. I guess because he was bigger than life, I've never been able to fully accept his death.

He was a war hero, a coach, a teacher, a loving father, a musician, and a singer with a voice you could hear in the next county. He was a religious man who, all his life, enjoyed a one-on-one relationship with his maker. He was a humorist whose stories could reduce any audience to howls and tears. He was, without any doubt, the funniest man I ever knew or heard of.

He was also an alcoholic, a con man, and a scalawag without peer. He fought bravely in two wars and in Korea; he was captured and held prisoner by the Chinese. Some people say that Lewis was forever scarred by his combat days. Talking with his boyhood friends, however, makes it quite apparent that Lewis was a rounder long before he put on the uniform of his country. Like every other Grizzard male I have ever known, he had great charm and a great thirst.

I don't know a great deal about the disease of alcoholism, but I know that Lewis had very strange drinking habits. While he was never able to win his battle with the bottle, he fought it every day of his life. I don't mean he resisted drinking; I mean he fought it harder than he had ever fought the Germans or the Chinese. He would go for as long as six months without a drink, but once he took that first one, he was on a long road that only went downhill.

He would do almost anything to keep his binge going. He would borrow, beg, tell any lie, or work any con to get one more drink. But even during his escapes into the bottle, his charm, personality, and humor would never leave him. He kept his face shaven, his shoes shined, and his clothes fresh. His full head of that Grizzard gray hair was always neatly cut, and he was the last man on earth you would ever suspect of any impropriety, let alone of being the world's foremost flimflam man looking to get his hands on your pocketbook.

But the truth is, no coffers were safe when Lewis was ready to tie one on.

As a younger man, Lewis was very active in his church. He was there every time they opened the door, and his rich voice filled that little country chapel. Of course, every member of the congregation was convinced that the Lord had sent him especially to their choir. He was also one of the members who took up the offering at Sunday worship service.

It had to happen that some money came up missing at about the same time Lewis came up missing. Everybody in the church was sure they knew where the money was, but they had no proof. Their conviction was based half on the fact that Lewis was missing, and half on his reputation.

They had a meeting to decide what steps, if any, should be taken. One dear lady pointed out that none of them knew for certain Lewis had taken the money, and even if they did, they should have Christian forgiveness in their hearts. They agreed they would all pray for whoever took the money.

In a few weeks, Lewis returned to town from his unexpected absence. He was back in the choir Sunday morning, and when the pastor said it was time for the offering, Lewis got out of his chair and passed the plate. Christian charity probably enjoyed its finest hour.

I first met Lewis while he was still in the Army. We were both at Uncle Frank's house, and Lewis was holding the hand of a small boy called Skipper. I was a teenager then and could never have guessed that Skipper and I would one day be closer than brothers, nor that the tall soldier would someday be my stepfather.

I did not see either one of them for several years. In fact, the next time I saw Lewis was at Uncle Frank's funeral in 1958. Like all Southern funerals, Uncle Frank's did not end at the cemetery. We all met afterwards for dinner and shared grief. Lewis had been divorced for many years, and my mother was a widow. It was easy for me to see that they enjoyed each other's company.

One thing led to another, and in a few months they were married. Lewis was working at Rich's, and there was no clue that he was not the pillar of the community. I was a young married man, and since my mother had always been my best friend, the four of us spent a lot of time together. We went on picnics, to football games, and to church together. For the first six months of their marriage I had never seen my mother happier. They loved each other very much, and it showed.

One night at dinner, Lewis announced that he had landed a job teaching at a private school in Atlanta. We knew how he loved teaching and were pleased at his good fortune. Some time later, I needed to talk to Lewis about some weekend plans we had made, so I called him at the private school. They had never heard of him.

It was a preview of things to come.

A wise man once wrote, "In the South, there are three kinds of drunks: lovin' drunks, fightin' drunks, and travelin' drunks." I happen to believe this is true. Lewis McDonald Grizzard, however, rarely traveled drunk. He was usually coming off one or on his way to get on one. He could cover more ground without a dime in his pocket than anybody since Christopher Columbus.

It took me a few years to get used to the fact that almost every time I heard from him, he was in a different city. He had no particular pattern to his travels, except that he stayed in the South. He would finance his sojourns however he could, and I'm sure he never allowed a shortage of funds to keep him from seeing what was around the next bend in the road.

When he was ready to stop for a few days or take a job for awhile, he usually chose a small town. He knew that small-town Southern people spoke his language, and given just a few hours, he could either find himself a job or talk someone out of some money.

If it was at all practical, he would try to take Skip along with him, much to the chagrin of Skip's mother. You would think that a man, broke or semi-broke and on the road if not on the lam, would not want the responsibility of a small boy. Not so with Lewis. He loved Skip so much that he would do almost anything to be with him.

Once, when Skip was about eight or nine years old, Lewis picked him up for the weekend. His mother was not to see him again for more than thirty days. Lewis talked to her every few days so she wouldn't be out of her mind with worry, and every time they spoke, he promised her that they were doing fine and would be home in a day or two. She knew better, but like the rest of the world, she was under his spell. She knew deep down that even though Lewis was the world's foremost rounder, he would never let anything happen to the Skipper.

On that particular trip, the two of them somehow wound up in Albany, Georgia, absolutely broke. Lewis noticed a sign in a store window announcing a minor league baseball game in town that night. Never one to allow a temporary lack of funds get in his way, he steered Skip straight to the ballpark and talked their way inside. They were watching batting practice when, the first thing Skip knew, his father was down on the field talking to one of the coaches. Albany was playing Waycross that night in the old Georgia-Florida league.

The record will never show how it happened, but record or no record, for the next month Lewis and Skip traveled with the Way-cross Braves. They rode the bus with the team and stayed with them on the road. Needless to say, Skip loved it. The team even gave him a little Waycross uniform. During the month of their baseball odyssey, Lewis borrowed money from the manager and the entire left side of the infield.

It was getting close to the start of Skip's school year, so he was returned to his worried mother.

One year, Lewis was teaching summer school in the tiny Georgia town of Tignal. He was living in the town's best boarding house, had joined the local church, and the townspeople thought he hung the moon. He was very much at home in lovely Tignal.

One afternoon, he took Skip by the hand and went to the home of the local school superintendent. He told the superintendent that he had to have some emergency dental work done the next day and asked if it would be possible to get an advance on his salary. The superintendent said, "Of course, Major Grizzard. That will be no problem at all." He gave Lewis the money on the spot.

The sun set, the Greyhound bus arrived and departed—along with Lewis, Skip, and the superintendent's money. As the bus made its way through the Georgia night, Lewis added the name of Tignal, Georgia, to a long list of towns he needed to avoid in the future.

When Skip was in high school, about six months went by when he didn't hear from his father. This was highly unusual because no matter how good or bad things were going for Lewis, he always managed to stay in touch with Skip.

Skip was on the basketball team, and one night the team was in Atlanta playing Headline High School. Skip was taking the ball down the court when he heard a familiar voice cheering for him from the stands. It was his daddy.

When the game was over, Skip ran up and asked, "Daddy, what on earth are you doing here?"

"I teach here," Lewis announced.

"What do you teach?" asked Skip.

"I teach mechanical drawing."

"Daddy," Skip pointed out, "You don't know anything about mechanical drawing."

"Thats true, son," Lewis said, smiling, "but neither do the students."

Of course, not all of Lewis and Skip's reunions were ideal. My company had transferred me to Birmingham, Alabama, and we had invited Lewis to come stay with us awhile to see if the change might help him get his act together. It seemed at the time that he might just be in the process of solving his drinking problem. He had not had a drink in several months, although, as usual, he was unwilling to stay on any job for more than a month or two. We had a spare bedroom, and I even had a spare car I offered to let him use. He moved in, and we were really glad to have him. My kids loved him, and, of course, he kept us laughing.

He had only been there a few days when he found a job at a small country club on the edge of town. It was perfect for him; he was a great manager, and the staff and members of the club soon fell under the spell of his great charm. He would come home every night laughing and telling us about his day. I only hoped it was not too good to be true. It was. The club closed for a month in the summer, but Lewis went in every day to make sure all was in order. When he didn't come home for three days, I told my wife that I was worried. I didn't want him to think I was checking on him, but I did want to find out what the hell was going on.

I called and let the phone ring about twenty times. I was about ready to hang up when a very young, very scared voice said, "Hello?"

I said, "May I speak to Mr. Grizzard, please?"

"He can't come to the phone now," the voice said.

I said thanks, I would call back, and was just about to hang up when the voice said, "Bob?" (That's my real name.)

It hit me all at once. "Skip!" I said.

"Boy! Am I glad to hear from you!" Skip practically hollered.

"Skipper," I asked, "what in the world are you doing in Birmingham?"

He told me the whole story.

Lewis had called Skip's mother and asked her to let him catch a bus and come to Birmingham. He gave her a tall tale about his new job and told her they were furnishing him with a nice place to live. He said that he and Skip could swim in the country club pool and spend some great time together. Skip's mother reminded him that Skip was only twelve years old and said she was worried about him going that far alone on a Greyhound bus. Lewis turned on the charm and assured her that he would meet Skip at the bus station and take wonderful care of him every minute.

With Lewis on one end of the line begging and Skip on the other end pleading, she never had a chance. I'm sure it was against her better judgment, but she finally agreed. She drove Skip from Moreland to Atlanta and put him on a Birmingham-bound bus. He was as excited as any twelve-year-old could be about seeing his daddy and all the fun they would have being alone at a great big country club.

When Skip got to the Birmingham bus station, he looked everywhere for the familiar face of his dad. No luck! He walked around and around the station, looking everywhere. When he was about ready to give up and was near tears, he heard his name being called on the public address system. He had a telephone call from Lewis, explaining that he had been delayed and directing Skip to take a taxi to the country club.

When Skip got to the club, he found his dad in bad shape. He was really drunk. He had unlocked the country club's liquor room and was playing the part of the Br'er Rabbit in the briar patch.

When I got Skip on the phone, he had been in Birmingham almost three days, and his daddy had been in a semi-drunken stupor most of the time. Whenever he would start to get sober, he would crawl right back in the bottle. Skip was pretty upset.

"Where is Lewis now?" I asked.

"He's passed out on a sofa in the lobby," said Skip.

I knew he was scared. I said, "Don't worry; I'm on my way. Everything will be all right."

Driving to the country club, I was furious. I was thinking how could he possibly bring that kid all the way over here and pull a stunt like this? I was also shocked that he would put the Skipper, whom I knew he loved above all things on earth, into such a horrible situation.

The country club was way out in the woods, and as I drove up the long dirt driveway, I wondered what I would find. Skip was on the porch waiting for me. He gave me the kind of hug you get only from a frightened youngster. He had been able to find a little to eat in the kitchen but had not had a full meal or a shower since he got there.

We went inside, and, sure enough, there was Lewis out cold on a big leather sofa. I told Skip to get his suitcase; we were going to my house to get him a meal and a bath.

"What about Daddy?" Skip asked.

I said, "Skip, right now I don't care much about what happens to him. We'll come back and see about him later."

I got Skip to my house, and got him fed, showered, and calmed down. Then my conscience started to bother me about leaving Lewis. I told Skip to come on—"Lets go back and see about your daddy." We drove back to the country club and went inside, fully expecting to find him still asleep on that sofa. But he was nowhere to be found. We searched every square inch of that clubhouse, but he had vanished.

Now I was really starting to worry. The car I had loaned him was in the parking lot, so we sat down to figure out where he might be. On a hunch, I called the nearest motel— about three miles away— figuring that if he had called a cab that was where he would go.

I had guessed right. The switchboard operator confirmed that Mr. Grizzard was registered. We got in my car and headed for the motel.

I approached the manager and asked for a key to Mr. Grizzard's room. The manager, a remarkably ill-tempered man, told me that if I did not get "that drunk" out of his motel, he was going to call the police. I explained to him in a loud voice that he had two options: he could call the police and not have his bill paid, or he could shut up, give me the room key, and let me try to get his guest in shape to travel. He gave me the key.

Skip and I went to the room and found Lewis comatose on the bed, an empty whiskey bottle on the table beside him. We shook him, tried to talk to him, but nothing helped. It was almost as if he were dead. I sent Skip out to get me a bucket of ice and poured it in the sink. I filled the sink with water, soaked a bath towel in the freezing liquid and put the cold, wet towel right in the middle of Lewis's ample stomach. He didn't even twitch. It became apparent to me that he was so drunk nothing we could do was going to get him on his feet. I finally decided that we were going to have to carry all 260 pounds of him to my car. I did not relish the thought of the Birmingham police carting Lewis off to jail.

I will never understand how, but we were able to get Lewis safely into the back seat of my car. I went by the motel office, turned in the key, paid the bill, told the snotty manager to kiss my ass, and left. With Lewis snoring loudly in the back seat, I drove home and parked in the carport so that my neighbors could not see my drunken cargo. I went in and told my wife what had happened and that I was taking Lewis to Atlanta. I was hoping that before we got there we would be able to get some food and coffee into him and decide what to do next. We started down Highway 78 with Lewis still snoring loudly in the back.

When we got to Cullman, Alabama, Skip said he was hungry, so we stopped. I sent him in to get some food we could eat in the car, and while Skip was getting our order filled, a deep voice came out of the back seat: "Robert? Robert? Are you there?"

"Yes, Lewis, I'm here."

"Robert, don't hate me."

"I don't hate you, Lewis."

"Are you mad at me, Robert?"

"Yes, Lewis, I'm mad at you."

"But you don't hate me?"

"No, Lewis, I don't hate you."

"Do you hate me just a little?"

"No, Lewis, I don't even hate you a little. Are you hungry, Lewis?"

"No, I may never eat again. Gully dirt doesn't get hungry, and I'm just as sorry as gully dirt. I don't deserve anything to eat."

"What do you want to eat, Lewis?" I asked.

"Two cheeseburgers and an order of fries."

I just couldn't do anything but laugh when I realized that, as drunk as he was, he was turning on that Grizzard charm.

When Skip got back with the food, Lewis was sitting up for the first time. He said, "Skipper, don't hate me."

"I don't hate you, Daddy."

"Do you hate me a little?"

"Lewis," I interrupted, "we don't hate you, but if you don't hush and eat, we're going to make you walk to Atlanta."

"*Walk* to Atlanta?" Lewis replied. "In the name of Gawd, Robert, I'd do good to get the car door open." We all cracked up, and I doubt if we quit laughing from Cullman to Atlanta.

Lewis wouldn't let me take him to my mother's house, but insisted I take him to his sister. When I let him out of the car, we gave each other a hug.

"Lewis, Lewis, Lewis," I chided him. "What is going to become of you?"

"You know me," he said. "I'll be all right."

God rest his soul, he never was.

I had been back in Birmingham about a week when the manager of the country club called me at my office. He was looking for "Major Grizzard." I said that I didn't know where Major Grizzard was, that the last time I saw him he was at his sister's house in Avondale Estates, Georgia.

"Well, he is not going to get away with this," the manager fumed.

"Get away with what?" I asked.

He went on to tell me that he had co-signed a note with Lewis at his bank for three hundred dollars. He was pretty angry and said again, "I trusted him, and I'll tell you one thing . . . he's not going to get away with this."

"Yes, he is," I countered.

"What?"

"Sir," I said, "I know how you must feel, and you have my sympathy, but the simple fact of the matter is he has gotten away with it. And you, sir, have just joined one of the largest fraternities in the Deep South. As a matter of curiosity," I went on, "how long did you know the Major before you signed a note with him?"

"Three days," he answered. "Why?"

"Just to see if, perchance, you held the record. You don't."

Lewis had been living in a small hotel in Gadsden, Alabama, for several weeks. He was eating his meals there and, of course, charging them to his room. The hotel didn't allow any bill to run more than a week, but like everyone else, the people there had been captivated by "the Major." The bill was about six weeks old before they started to press for their money.

Lewis gave them a check for his bill, and, of course, the check bounced higher than a nine-iron shot. Due to a serious miscalculation on Lewis's part, he was clearing the city limits about the same time his check was not clearing the bank. He was apprehended and put in a very unpleasant small-town jail. Allowed one telephone call, he called his boyhood friend, Harold, in Snellville. He filled the long distance line with charm and lies, and in a matter of a couple of hours, Harold was on his way to Alabama to help Lewis.

The police would not even talk to Harold about bail until he made the check to the hotel good, so Harold paid off the bad check and then posted Lewis's bail. Lewis was a free man.

Outside the jail, Lewis explained to poor Harold that he was innocent and the whole thing had been a serious mistake on the part of the local police. He went on to say that he was on his way to west Alabama where a job as a schoolteacher was waiting for him. He also mentioned that if Harold could help with a small loan, he, Lewis, would be able to complete his journey and rent an apartment. It would be a perfectly easy matter to get the money back to him in a few days. The bottom line is, Lewis was able to talk Harold out of five hundred dollars, an incredible amount of money in those days.

Harold returned to Snellville having paid off a bad check, paid Lewis's bond, and given him five hundred dollars in cash. A true good Samaritan was about to learn a very expensive lesson. He waited patiently for his money; as far as I know, he's still waiting.

It's hard to imagine how Lewis was able to pull off such a scam with someone he had known all his life. Harold knew that Lewis was completely untrustworthy. He had to know that he was never going to get a dime of his money back. So why would he do it?

The truth is, it was almost impossible to say no to the Major—even when you knew that he was about to separate you from your bankroll. Lewis had a distant northern cousin whom he had seen only once or twice in his life. She had won $16,000 on "The $64,000 Question," and she and her husband used part of their winnings to visit their relatives in Georgia.

When they left, Skip said to Lewis, "Boy! Daddy, they sure have a lot of money."

Lewis smiled big and said, "Not as much as they came with."

Skip didn't know what he meant at the time, but it's certainly clear now that it was just another case of Lewis talking his way into someone's heart and pocketbook.

There was also the time when Skip was in his second year at the University of Georgia and Lewis came through Athens for a short visit. Skip introduced Lewis to his roommate in passing, a brief exchange lasting only long enough for Lewis to find out that the young man was from Cordele, Georgia.

The next time Lewis found himself in Cordele, broke, he remembered Skip's roommate's name, called him, and borrowed some money—even though it was *six years* later.

But probably the best example of how hard it was to say no to Lewis is the story of Skip's best friend in high school, Ron Jenkins. Ron had never met Lewis until, one day, Lewis dropped in and Skip introduced them. Ron was about seventeen years old at the time and was naturally taken with Lewis's hilarious stories and great charm.

Later, when they were alone, Skip took Ron aside and gave him a warning: "Sooner or later, maybe a week, maybe a year, Daddy is going to call you and try and borrow some money from you. No matter what you do, don't let him have it, because you will never get it back." Ron said he understood.

About a year had gone by when Ron got a telephone call: "Ronny, my boy, I just got into town and thought about how much I enjoyed your company the last time we met. I was wondering if you could meet me at Lucille's for a visit? I sure would enjoy seeing you again."

Of course, Ron was flattered that Lewis wanted to see him again, but Skip's words still echoed in his head: "Don't lend him any money."

Lucille's Place was not a bar, nor a lounge, nor was it a pub. Lucille's Place was a beer joint. Before Ron left, he took five dollars out of his wallet. He remembered Skip's warning and was going to take no chances.

They had a few beers together, and before long everybody in the beer joint was gathered around their table laughing and whooping as Lewis told one funny story after another. Before he left, every person there agreed that he was the funniest man on the face of the earth.

When Ron and Lewis decided to call it a night, Lewis said, "Ronny, I wonder if you could do me a small favor. You see, I am on my way to Atlanta to pick up a car from my brother. I'm then driving to North Carolina to accept a job as headmaster at a very exclusive private school. The school some-how bungled my travel allowance, and I was wondering if you could let me have a few dollars. I'll be able to send it back to you as soon as I get to the school."

Ron knew that there was not a word of truth in the story, and he damn well knew that he was never going to get his money back. Nevertheless, he went home, got his last fifty bucks, and turned it over to Lewis.

In doing the legwork for this book, I asked Ron what he thought about the incident after all these years.

"Without any doubt," he said, "it was the best investment I ever made."

It was also nearly impossible to stay mad at Lewis, no matter what he had done to you. What it boils down to is: to know Lewis was to love him—not just like him, but really love him. I don't know where old Harold is today, but I can assure you that, like Ron, he has long since forgiven Lewis, and like me, he would give anything for just five minutes of the Major's company.

During one of his down times, Lewis was staying for a few days with his brother Frank and Aunt Jill. Aunt Jill did not trust banks and often kept a lot of cash around the house. Her own past experience dictated, however, that when Lewis was coming to visit, all cash had to be very well hidden.

Aunt Jill's house looked like it had been decorated from the midway at the Southeastern Fair, and she had a large Mexican sombrero hanging on the wall of the living room. It was inside that big old Mexican hat that she decided to hide her sixteen hundred dollars. God only knows how, but Lewis found the money and was gone like Jimmy Hoffa.

The next time anybody heard from him, he was in Little Rock, Arkansas, very broke, very hung over, and very remorseful. Uncle Frank and Aunt Jill drove to Little Rock to pick him up. They took him home to recover from his binge, and as far as I know, they never mentioned the sixteen hundred dollars to him.

You don't get mad at a fish for swimming, and you didn't get mad at Lewis for ripping you off. There was just something in the Grizzard genes, as I understood even more clearly when I met Lewis and Frank's brother Wesley.

Wesley was, of course, just as charming as the rest of his family. He had spent his entire life selling cars, and when I was about twenty-five, my family was growing and I decided I needed a station wagon. I mentioned that fact to Lewis, and he called Wesley to see if perhaps there were a good buy on a second-hand station wagon to be had at his current place of employment. Wesley assured Lewis that the cream puff of all cream puffs was on his lot, and he would let it go at a tiny fraction of its value. So we drove to a used car lot with the high-sounding name of Belvedere Motors.

The station wagon in question was about ten years old and looked like it had spent all ten years on a taxi line. It was rough, but since I didn't want to hurt Wesley's feelings, I agreed to take it on a test drive. I drove, Wesley sat in the front seat, and Lewis was in the back seat. The car rattled so loudly that it was hard to talk over the noise.

When I mentioned all the noise to Wesley, he said, "Oh, that's easy to fix," and he reached over and turned up the radio. With a great deal of satisfaction in his voice he said, "Now, then . . . that's better."

I turned on the heater and the roar was deafening. It sounded like somebody was under the hood tearing a cat in half.

"Does that heater sound funny to you?" Uncle Wesley asked. When I agreed that it did, he said, "I'm sure a slight adjustment will fix that little problem."

When we got back to Belvedere Motors, I raised the hood and saw oil everywhere. Without missing a beat, Wesley said, "A little steam cleaning, and she'll look just like new."

I told him that I would have to think
about it. He offered to sell it to me for twenty-
five dollars down. I didn't tell him, but I had
serious doubts that it was worth twenty-five
dollars total.

When we started home, Lewis said,
"Now, Wesley is my brother and I love him,
but when it comes to buying a car from him,
old Wesley will bear watching."

You talk about the pot calling the kettle
black.

But the truly wonderful thing about
Lewis was that he was always somehow able
to have fun, no matter where he went or how
hard times were. He had fun, and if you were
with him, you had fun. He could turn a simple trip to a high school basketball game
into an adventure that you would remember
forever.

If Lewis loved anything, he loved to put
people on. He could pull off most of his
stunts because he could keep a straight face
and he absolutely exuded authority. It may
have come from his years as an Army officer,
coach, and teacher. He gave the impression
that he was an important man, and with his
quiet self-assurance, most people never
thought to doubt him.

I had to go to Milledgeville, Georgia, on
an overnight business trip, and since Lewis
was between jobs, I asked him to go with

me. As soon as we got to Milledgeville, we checked into our hotel and Lewis bought a local newspaper. He suddenly exclaimed, "This is wonderful! There's a high school basketball game tonight. Let's go!"

"Who's playing?" I asked.

"What difference does it make?" he answered. "All high school games are wonderful. We'll go early, eat hot dogs for supper, and see the girls' game and the boys' game. It will be a marvelous evening."

I don't know many people who could resist a "marvelous" evening with Lewis, so we showered, shaved, and set out for the local high school gym. There were no parking places in the school lot, and we had to drive around the area to find a spot. We walked about two blocks to the gym, and the way he was carrying on, you would have thought we were going to the Super Bowl instead of a high school game where we didn't even know who was playing.

When we arrived at the gym, I offered to stand in the long line that had formed and buy the tickets.

"That won't be necessary," Lewis said. "Come with me."

"But we don't have any tickets," I pointed out.

"Come along, Robert," he said, ignoring my protest. "We mustn't be late." We walked up to the door where a young teacher in his late twenties was taking up tickets. We were on our way past him when he said, "Tickets, please."

Lewis stopped, looked him over from head to toe, turned to me, and in his best Major Grizzard voice said, "Robert, who is this person?"

I said, "He's the ticket taker."

"I see," Lewis said, and with that we turned and walked into the gym, leaving the man standing there wondering what he had done wrong.

We had our supper of hot dogs, French fries, and Cokes. We watched the girls' game, and Lewis cheered for Milledgeville like he had daughters on the team. The gym was starting to fill up as the time for the boys' game got closer. Lewis was seated on the aisle and had everybody around us laughing at his running commentary.

Two students who appeared to be in about eighth grade walked up the aisle, and when Lewis saw them, he summoned them over to his seat.

"Boys," he demanded in his best teacher's voice, "who is your homeroom teacher?"

Honest to God, the poor boys practically came to attention as they spouted out the answer.

"Why are you boys not wearing stockings?" was Lewis's next question, and the boys just stood there bewildered. "Are you boys accustomed to coming to school functions looking like ragamuffins? If you don't have any pride in yourselves, you must take some pride in your school."

"Yes, sir," they said, their eyes lowered in shame.

"Now," continued Lewis, "I want you two boys to go to the front door and tell the teacher there that Mr. Grizzard is sending you home to put on your stockings, and that he is to let you in when you get back. And, boys, don't ever let me see you at any school function again without your stockings on. Do you understand me, boys?"

"Yes, sir, Mr. Grizzard," they said remorsefully. "We understand."

"Boys," Lewis concluded, "you must always seek to bring credit to your school as well as your mothers and fathers. Now hurry home before you miss the game." They just stood there with their mouths slightly ajar until Lewis added, "You can go now, boys . . . go . . . go!" Then they sprinted up the aisle.

There is, of course, no way to tell for sure, but I believe with all my heart that wherever those two young men are today, they are wearing their stockings, thereby bringing credit to their mothers and fathers.

Lewis McDonald Grizzard, Sr., was born on August 5, 1912. He died on August 12,

1970. I was in Savannah on business, in a client's office, when the call came. I made my apologies and walked outside to one of those beautiful little parks that dot the Savannah streets. I sat down on a park bench, and before I knew it, was crying like a child into my handkerchief.

It has been more than twenty years since that day, and when I think of him now, it is with a mixture of happiness and sadness. The happiness comes from remembering the grand times we had together, his great funny stories, and the laughter we shared. I smile when I remember him at the piano—this giant of a man tearing up a piano and singing gospel music at the top of his lungs. I smile when I remember how people were drawn to his magic personality, how he would have dinner in a restaurant and make twenty new friends before it was time for dessert. I chuckle when I think of the outrageous stories he would tell of his childhood in Snellville. I feel warm all over when I remember how anytime we parted or met, he would hug me. I laugh when I remember the times we went to the grocery store at midnight for buttermilk, fresh bread and red hots. Lewis called it our twelve o'clock snack. It was impossible to be around him without feeling good about him, yourself, and the human race in general.

I also think, sometimes, about his life-long struggle with alcohol. It was the biggest battle of his life, and one he was never able to win. The bottle caused most of the problems in his life: the divorces, the bad checks, the lies, and the broken promises. The sadness I still feel is for the terrible waste. Here was a man who could have owned the world, a man who could have been an earthshaking success at anything he tried. Here was the potential legend — good, kind, and immensely talented — but a man who could never survive long between drinks. The waste is, by far, the saddest part.

Lewis died in the tiny Georgia town of Claxton. A stroke had stopped that huge heart one week shy of his fifty-eighth birthday. Skip was sitting at his bedside holding his hand when he took his last breath. Lewis's sole possessions on that hot Georgia night were a watch, a ring, and a Georgia driver's license.

The funeral was held in Lawrenceville with burial in the family plot at the Zior Church. I remember thinking as I carried his flag-draped coffin to the gravesite, "I hope this wonderful man has at long last found peace. Please, God, grant him that."

The passing years have not changed my memories of Lewis. I know and accept what he was. I still grieve about what he could have been. In the years we knew each other, there were times I loved him and times I wanted to pull his head off. There was never, however, a time when I did not enjoy the pleasure of his company.

I will remember him always.

Skip Grizzard: Poor Little Rich Boy

To his legion of fans throughout the world, Skip Grizzard probably embodies the American dream—famous, wealthy, wildly successful. Duty compels me, however, to tell the other side of the story. Skip is a man for whom practically nothing has gone right.

Except for his adventures with his father, Skip had a pretty typical childhood. He did what most small-town Southern children did. In the winter, he went to school, did his homework, and when forced to do so, took care of a few chores around the house. He looked forward to Christmas, Thanksgiving, and any sporting event that he could pick up on his small, table-model Zenith radio.

In the summertime, he liked to loaf a lot. He would go swimming when he could or play baseball with his friends whenever they could gather enough for a game. He rarely missed an Atlanta Crackers game on his Zenith.

He learned early on that as an only child, there were times when he had to entertain himself. He would pass many hours standing in his yard, hitting small rocks with a stick, and pretending he was a baseball announcer calling his imaginary game. He would hit a rock and then do the play-by-play: "Montag hits a screamer down the line . . . it's going all the way to the fence . . . it's a stand-up double for Bob Montag!"

His interest in sports developed early and has only intensified over the years. He liked peanuts, Coca-Cola, and all his mama's cooking. He enjoyed everything that most other little boys enjoyed, and like most other little boys, he didn't like girls.

During the summer between fifth and sixth grade, Skip was attending Vacation Bible School. It was here that Skip Grizzard first met Nancy Carroll. There were no fireworks, no violins in the background, just a little boy meeting a little girl for the first time.

One of Skip's friends asked him if he thought Nancy would be in their class when school started in September. Skip said, "I hope not, 'cause she sure is ugly."

Time has a way of changing things, and by the time Nancy was thirteen, she was a beauty. When Skip and Nancy were both that age, they went on a hayride sponsored by the Baptist Training Union. It was not a date; they just both happened to be along. When they passed slowly alongside Bear Creek, Nancy reached over and kissed Skip. Skip remembers it not as a little peck, but a real, grown-up kiss. This time, the fireworks and violin music started.

When the evening was over, Skip said to himself, "I've got to marry this one." The romance started that night and continued on through high school. They would fight and break up, usually because of jealousy over another boy or another girl. Nancy, like Skip, was an only child, and they had enough in common and enough love between them that they always seemed to make up.

People who went to high school with Nancy still agree that she was pretty, sexy, radiant, and, most of all, happy. One classmate says she was everybody's idea of what the "girl next door" should be.

While her high school relationship with Skip has been described as rocky, there is not much doubt that when they were happy, they made Ozzie and Harriet look like two drill instructors. In spite of their frequent spats and make-ups, their relationship continued to grow. They became not only sweethearts, but, by the time they finished high school, best buddies. They were both nineteen on their wedding day. It was one of those marriages that you knew would last forever. It had so much going for it that it was hard to even conceive of its demise. Here were two bright, attractive people with their entire lives in front of them. God had not only given them looks and talent; he had made them best friends. Skip and Nancy had a huge head start on most newlyweds. Their ace in the hole was they were deeply in love, crazy in love, let's-hold-hands in love.

But marriage to Nancy was one of Skip's early lessons that things don't always work out the way you plan. The romance that had started on a hayride when they were both thirteen ended in a divorce court when they were both twenty-two. It was a day that has never been far from Skip's mind. I have never discussed the marriage or divorce with Nancy, but have spent many sad hours talking about it with Skip.

In the years since their divorce, Skip has married two lovely women and has been involved to one degree or another with many, many others. When you asked what happened to his other marriages and the other relationships, you get answers running from Skip's partying to his roving eye. I don't know all the answers, but let me give you one fact that you can take to the bank. Skip loves Nancy as much today as he did on their wedding day. Every woman to pass through his adult life has been compared to Nancy. I'm not saying he didn't love both of his other wives. Only Skip can handle that one. I do know in my own heart that Nancy was the Big Love of his life, maybe so big that there has been little room left over for the others.

In a quiet moment recently, Skip and I were having dinner together in a restaurant. The subject of Nancy came up, and Skip said, "If God would allow me to do one thing over, you know what it would be?"

"What?" I asked.

"I would have treated Nancy better. I would be so good to her that we would never be anything except happy." Looking up from the tablecloth where he had been staring, he added, "Ya see, Lud, I'll always be in love with her."

I believe him, I really do. It just didn't always seem that way at the time.

It was the summer of 1969, not long after Skip and Nancy had come to Atlanta and settled into their lovely home in DeKalb County, and Skip was invited to go see the Braves play Cincinnati. He was going to the game with his fellow sportswriter and friend, Frank Hyland. He told Nancy that he would be home as soon as the game was over. It turned out that the game was one of the fastest in major league history, and by about nine-thirty Frank and Skip found themselves in the parking lot of Atlanta-Fulton County Stadium with a great thirst and some time on their hands.

They decided that they would stop off for a quick cocktail and then go straight home. It goes without saying that they had several cocktails and did not resume their trip home until shortly after two in the morning. En route home, they were delayed at a railroad crossing by the passing of a long freight train. Such a long train, in fact, that they both fell asleep while waiting there and didn't wake up until after five o'clock. Since Skip had to be at work by six or six-thirty, and since Nancy would be waiting, time became of the essence.

When they arrived at Skip's formerly happy home, they found that sometime during the evening or early morning hours, Nancy had thrown all of Skip's clothes into the front yard. They weren't sure what this meant, but assumed that Nancy might be expressing some displeasure at Skip's failure to return home. She had also locked all the doors and would not let him in the house. The clock was ticking, and he was afraid he was going to be late for work, so he was forced to change his clothes in his front yard.

Obviously, Skip hadn't intended to get home at five-thirty in the morning; things just didn't work out like he planned.

The same can be said for his several attempts to get back together with Nancy after they had separated — they didn't go quite as intended either. One such attempt took place when Skip was living with his buddy Ron Hudspeth. Ron was newly divorced, and Skip was on his own, so they decided that they were going to be swinging singles. They rented a nice place at the Red Lion Apartments and furnished it with what little furniture Ron had. All Skip had was his clothes, a portable typewriter, and a toothbrush that was badly in need of repair. He had to rent a bed and mattress. Actually, the place looked like something straight out of *The Grapes of Wrath.*

Ron came home one day to find Skip sitting on the floor watching a small black-and-white TV set. He was surrounded by empty beer cans and using a muffin tin as an ashtray (there were no real ashtrays in the apartment). He had been sitting there all day drinking beer and smoking Marlboro cigarettes, and he was wearing his best hang-dog look. He was not at all happy being a swinging single. His only thoughts were of Nancy sitting in their spotlessly clean home. He imagined that she was dressed like Loretta Young, with long dangling earrings and that honey blonde hair, bright and shiny and hanging down around her shoulders. He would go in, their eyes would meet, they would kiss, and she would say, "My darling . . . I've missed you so much." They would kiss again and live happily ever after.

He was right in the middle of his fantasy, sitting there on the floor, when Ron came in. Skip looked at him and said, "I'm going back to Nancy, and if you try and stop me, I'll kill you." He got in his car and headed to home sweet home. All he could think about was how beautiful Nancy would look and how they would rekindle that old flame. It never occurred to him that he might be wasting a trip.

He opened the front door just as Nancy was coming out of the kitchen. She was wearing an old ratty housecoat. She had no makeup on, and her hair was in curlers. When she saw Skip, she offered the time-honored greeting: "What the hell do you want?"

In less than an hour, Skip was back on the floor at the fancy Red Lion apartment, watching TV with his muffin tin at his side. There are some days when you should stay in bed.

That was not the only time Skip tried without success to return to Nancy. Another time, he had fallen in love with a beauty in Montreal while there covering a Braves series. When he got back to Atlanta, it was more than obvious that Mr. Cupid had kicked him right in the belly. The only thing he could talk about was his Canadian beauty—their candlelit suppers, their evenings together. This woman, he vowed, was the love of his life. He called her; he wrote her beautiful love letters. When he could stand it no longer, he took his vacation, and since he was terrified of flying, he set out by car for Montreal and the girl he left behind.

The rest of his trip is a little cloudy. She did not look as pretty as he had remembered. The candlelit supper did not live up to expectations, and besides, she had a boyfriend. After a hard-fought screaming match, Skip got in his car and started back South. He drove straight back. I don't know how far it is from Atlanta to Montreal, but I know it's one killer of a trip. On the long drive home, fantasies about getting back together with Nancy started to rumble around in his head again. By the time he got back to Atlanta, he was absolutely convinced that he could patch things up if he could just talk to her for five minutes.

He got to Atlanta at about 3:00 a.m. and decided that there was no time like the present. He went straight to Nancy's house. Her car was there, but she was not at home. He sat down in his car to wait. He lit a cigarette, and his thoughts went something like this:

"Where the hell could she be? I mean, for God's sake, it's three o'clock in the morning. She should be at home at three-a-damn-clock in the morning. Who could she be with? I'll tell you who she's with . . . she's with a man on a date—that's who she's with. Wait till she gets here. I'll teach that home-wrecking SOB to date my wife. . . . But wait—suppose he's a great big old home wrecking SOB?" With this thought, he got out of his car, opened the trunk and took out his lug wrench, and got back into his car, ready to do battle.

Nothing much ever turns out like Skip wants it to. When the sun came up, he decided it was time to go home. He found out later that Nancy had spent the night with a girlfriend. But his fierce determination to take vengeance that night has been forever memorialized at the Atlanta newspapers as "Grizzard's Lug Wrench Syndrome."

On the
Wide Path

As a matter of fact, Skip claims that even his career, as successful as it seems, is far from what he intended. The truth is, his first great ambition was to write pornographic books for a living. He was eighteen years old and was at the home of his high school friend Ron Jenkins. They were drinking Ancient Age and trying to come up with some ideas about how to raise money for college.

They rejected such ideas as working at the peach shed or trying to get a summer job with the county. As the level of the bourbon bottle went down, the level of their creativity seemed to go up. They talked about going to Florida, buying seafood, bringing it to Atlanta, and selling it for a huge profit. This idea was rejected when they realized that neither one of them owned a car or a cooler. They briefly considered becoming bootleggers, but then concluded that while they knew a great deal about drinking it, they knew nothing about making it.

Then it hit them like a pulpwood truck. Of all the folks on the face of the earth, who knew more about porno than Ron and Skip? After all, they had both read every porno book available to an eighteen-year-old in Coweta County.

It was foolproof. They could make enough for college with one book. College, hell! They could be multimillionaires.

More Ancient Age, more plans. They decided the best thing to do was to move to Key West, where they would buy a house on the beach and turn out a book every week.

Suddenly Ron said, "This ain't never going to work."

Skip said, "Of course it'll work. What about all that money? It'll work . . . it'll work."

"What about our mamas?" Ron asked. "It'll just kill our mamas. If they knew we knew all that stuff, let alone wrote a book about it. . . . What about the preacher? I know he don't see a lot of us, but he sure knows who we are. We would disgrace both of our families."

They had another drink and tried to think of a way around their problem. After a few minutes, Skip jumped all the way out of his chair and shouted, "I got it! We'll use a fake name."

"Oh, like a *nom de plume*," Ron offered.

"No, a fake name," said Skip.

It was now decision time. What name would do justice to the classic pornographic literature they were all set to mass produce? They rejected "Harlow Horney" and "Rex Sex" as too undignified. They decided to put their real names together and see if they could come up with a combination worthy of their great talents. They wrote out their names on a piece of Blue Horse notebook paper: Ronald Shaddix Jenkins and Lewis McDonald Grizzard. They tried the letters in every possible combination and, after one more drink, decided their pen name would be Shadron Lumac.

When the sun came up the next morning, they decided that the idea, without the Ancient Age, lacked merit. But I don't know. I've always been a little sad that Shadron Lumac died before he made it to Key West.

But be that as it may, once that aspiration flickered out, Skip did a complete about-face. (I should mention here that in researching this book, I interviewed Skip at great length. In most cases, I found that his memory was in serious conflict with the memory of his friends.) He told me that when he first came to Atlanta from college to work for the Atlanta newspapers, it was only to be a temporary job until he could get into the ministry full time. He said his plans were to pastor a small church in Gwinnett County and to look after the needs of his flock. He claimed that had he not fallen into the bad company of newspapermen, he would have spent many wonderful nights at deacon meetings and eaten fried chicken on the grounds every Sunday. He further claims that had he not met or been forced to work with this rowdy element, he could have built the Doublewide Church of Gwinnett into a mighty cathedral with members from Lawrenceville to Zior. Of course, Nancy would have made the perfect preacher's wife.

Well, it didn't turn out that way. Whether because of the influence of his rowdy colleagues or for some other reason, Skip decided to leave the straight and narrow and to follow the wide path.

For Skip, the wide path usually led to women. He and his friend Ron Jenkins developed womanizing into an absolute science. They were both young single guys (this is after Skip's divorce from Nancy) in their mid-twenties in the big city of Atlanta. They both had jobs, and they both worked hard at them. If, however, they had spent as much time on their jobs as they did chasing every available woman in the five-county metro area, they would be very wealthy men today. I am convinced that during that period of their lives, had you hit either one of them in the head with an axe, millions of tiny women would have come spilling out—all sizes, shapes, and colors.

I would go to lunch with them, and the conversation would go something like this:

Ludlow: " Well, how's everything going?"

Skip: "Take a look at the blonde in the corner booth."

Ron: "I love her and want to spend eternity at her side."

Skip: "The waitress ain't bad either!"

Ron: "Ain't bad? She's beautiful! I love her and want to spend eternity at her side."

Skip: "Did you see the hostess as we came in?"

Ron: "You mean the redhead? God, is she something! I love her and want to spend eternity at her side."

Skip: "We got this new girl at the paper."

Ron: "I love her and want to spend eternity at her side."

Skip: "No you don't. She's a real dog."

Ron: "I bet she's got a roommate that I could love and spend eternity at her side."

Ludlow: "There seems to be a severe grease fire in the kitchen."

Skip: "Do they have women firefighters in Atlanta?"

Ron: "If they do, I will love them and spend eternity at their side."

There was a strict code of conduct among these intrepid woman-chasers. If circumstances caused one of them to leave, without the other, because he had talked someone into something, he was not to be criticized, even if he took the car and the other was left on foot.

If Skip told a woman that he was a doctor by the name of Blake Funderburk, it was up to Ron to not only back up his story, but to call him Blake or Dr. Funderburk for the balance of the evening. If Ron told a woman that they were businessmen in town from

Boston for a convention, it was up to Skip to do a John Kennedy impression as long as the young lady in question was within earshot.

Skip and Ron began networking years before the word was in common usage. Tuesday was a special day in their constant quest. Tuesday was set aside for what they referred to as "research and development." Rule number one was "No sex on Tuesday, no matter what." Here is the way it worked:

On Tuesday afternoon about five or six o'clock, our two heroes would go to a local watering hole called The Rising Sun, known to draw a great crowd of women. They were not there, however, to pick up women; they were there to get a supply of new names and new telephone numbers to get them through the upcoming week. The M.O. was beautiful in its simplicity. They would find a woman and strike up a conversation with her. No advances were made except at the conclusion of the conversation, which went something like this: "I've enjoyed talking to you. You are a breath of fresh air after talking to so many bubbleheads all week. It sure is nice to run into an attractive woman with brains. I don't want to appear forward, but I'd like to buy your lunch one day. May I call you at work?"

What could be more innocent? They were careful not to ask for a home phone number, and they didn't try to make a date for after dark. It would just be an amiable lunch with two intellectuals exchanging ideas. It worked almost every time. Once they had the phone number and name written down, they shook hands, excused themselves and disappeared into the crowd to find another woman to give the same line to. It was not uncommon at all for each of them to have ten names and numbers by the end of the night. The next step was to transfer the information they had obtained from bar napkins to large index cards.

They could evaluate the success of their Tuesday night research only when all of the index cards were spread out in front of them. A card not only contained a woman's name and phone number; it also included her physical attributes and some personal comments by the researchers.

"Great body," a comment might read, "cute face, brain appears to be completely inoperative. Told her my cousin was Queen Elizabeth, and she said, 'Oh really? What does she do?' "

When all the information was organized and filed, it was time to go to work. The first target was called, and a day and place arranged for the "innocent" lunch. Then, on the appointed day, Skip or Ron would call and tell her something like this:

"I'm really sorry to call you at the last minute, but I'm not going to be able to make lunch. The mayor called, and I'm going to be stuck in his office all day advising him about the new expressway system. I've been looking forward to lunch all week, and I was just wondering if we could change it to dinner tonight? . . . You will? That's wonderful! . . . What's your address? And you had better give me that old home phone number, too, just in case I get lost."

Not a bad scam. The innocent lunch had now been turned into a dinner-date, with visions of king-sized beds dancing in Skip's and Ron's heads. Even after the index cards were used, they still had value. They could either be kept for future reference or bought and sold like shares on the New York Stock Exchange.

If Ron and Skip's attitude sounds sexist, that's because it was. Sex was a game, and to play it, you needed women; pretty women if possible, but in a pinch just about any women. And like any other game they played, it was necessary to have contests and keep score.

On one occasion, they had a bet on how many women they could bed down in forty-eight hours. Ron won, nine to eight. In commenting on his victory years later, Ron said, "Skip got arrogant after eight, and I was able to take advantage of his attitude and move by him in the closing minutes."

Not all of their sexual contests had time limits. When Ron was still in his twenties and selling real estate in Atlanta, he vowed to make love to every operator at his answering service. It took him almost a year, but he vows to this day that his efforts were well rewarded — if not in quality, certainly in quantity.

In the interest of honesty and fair play, I should point out here that Ron has been happily married for many years and now owns an answering machine.

Of course, given Skip's inclination toward misfortune, you can bet that his life in the fast lane produced a fair number of blown tires. At one point during the post-Nancy era, he was living with several rowdy roommates in a fashionable Cobb County apartment about twenty miles from downtown Atlanta. He put in long hours at the paper, and one hectic night, as he was working away long after midnight, he started picturing the six-pack of beer and the hunk of his favorite cheese waiting for him in his refrigerator. By the time he finished work, all he could think about was getting home, settling back in his recliner, eating his cheese, and putting a serious dent into that frosty, delicious six-pack. The only thing that could add to his pleasure was if the SuperStation were showing a John Wayne western or a Warner Brothers gangster picture.

He got to his car about 2:15, dead tired and as thirsty as a prairie dog. He kept thinking to himself, "Just a few more minutes until I can relax, sip beer, nibble that wonderful cheese, and doze." He said a silent prayer that his rowdy roomies would be asleep. The last thing he wanted was any company or conversation. The trip home was like waiting for Christmas.

When he finally pulled into his parking place, the vision of his chair, his cheese, and his beer loomed larger than a Cecil B. De-Mille movie. He dragged his way up the concrete steps, walked into his apartment, and froze. Sitting in his living room and drinking his beer were two African-American women wearing micro-mini skirts, skin-tight sequined blouses, and platform shoes with heels like step ladders.

"Who are you and what are you doing here?" Skip asked.

The one in his chair said, "We're working girls, honey. Who are you?"

Skip stormed into his roommates' bedroom all set to kill. There he found two of his colleagues passed out cold. They had obviously been in a heavyweight bout with the bottle and had lost. He shook them, pinched them, and poured water on them. Nothing helped. They were down for the long count, and barring a religious miracle, nothing was going to wake either one of them up, except time.

He returned to the living room just in time to see one of the hookers finish the last bite of his cheese.

"Okay," he demanded, "what's the story? How did you all get here?" He stood there grieving over his lost beer and cheese and heard the whole sorry saga. His roommates had picked the women up as they worked the street outside the Sans Souci Lounge. They had been promised dining, dancing, and riches beyond their wildest dreams. Once inside the car, they were taken to the apartment in Cobb County where both of their hosts promptly passed out. So here they were, twenty miles from their working area, with no dinner, no dancing, no money — just a six-pack of beer and some Kraft processed cheese. "Well, you two have got to get out of here," Skip told them.

"Where the hell we goin', man? We ain't got a dime and don't even know where we are. Who's goin' to pay us for our valuable time? And who's goin' to take us back to the Sans Souci?"

Skip's mind raced. He thought of and rejected several schemes to get rid of his unwanted guests. He made a mental note to kill his roommates as soon as he could come up with an alibi. He finally told the two hookers that he had no money, but if they would go quietly, he would drive them back to their working area. They didn't like not being paid, but after some discussion, they agreed that a ride back to town was as good as they were going to do.

Skip packed them into his 1968 Cutlass, and, with the faint aroma of his beer and cheese making his stomach ache with emptiness, they started on their journey.

They were no more than out of the parking lot when a horrible thought went through his mind: "What if I'm involved in a horrible accident and we're all killed? What will the preacher say at my funeral? He will have to tell the truth. I can hear him now — 'Brother Grizzard was called home while in the company of two harlots.' My mother will never be able to hold her head up in Moreland, Georgia, again. The paper will deny that I ever worked there, and those two drunks back at the apartment will refuse to be my pallbearers. I'd just better drive carefully," he told himself.

Then he thought, "What if I get stopped by the police? I can see the headlines now: 'Skip Grizzard suspected of being a pimp . . . Grizzard gets five years on a no beer and cheese diet.' I've got to pull myself together," he thought. "The only thing I've got to be sure of is that nobody sees me let these two out of my car."

He was well known at the Sans Souci and was worried about being spotted as he stopped to discharge his passengers. He took a deep breath and said, "Ladies, when we get in front of the Sans Souci, I'm going to slow down to five miles per hour. When I say, 'Now,' I want you to open the door and jump."

"Hey, man," said the one next to the door, "we ain't jumpin' out of no damn movin' car."

"If you don't," Skip told them, "you're going right back to Cobb County."

The hooker in the middle turned to her friend and said, "I told you, Bethaka, we got to start a union."

"I heard that," said her friend.

Suffice it to say that Skip safely made his drop and returned to his sleeping room-mates in Cobb County—both of whom, by the way, are now well-known names in the Atlanta media, long since married, and semi-settled down. I can't tell you their names, because if either one of them ever writes a book, I don't want to be in it.

(I don't really think that Skip's habit of keeping bad company really kept him out of the ministry. In fact, given some of the recent scandals involving television preachers, he might have fit right in.)

Honesty compels me to report, also, that despite his considerable success with the fairer sex, Skip has occasionally come up with an empty sack. Sometimes it was his fault; sometimes circumstances did him in.

Skip fell in love, once, with a young librarian who was as proper as a prayer meeting. She was what everybody pictured a librarian to be: glasses, hair up in a bun, and she spoke the King's English like it was meant to be spoken. There wasn't a word of slang in her vocabulary. She did not smoke, drink, or have any bad habits. In short, she was a lady.

Frankly, I never knew what the attraction was. She was beautiful, but not very good company, and she certainly didn't seem like Skip's type.

Skip and two of his rowdy friends had rented a luxury apartment on the edge of town, and he was very proud of his new abode. One afternoon, he talked the librarian into going to his place for dinner. He had painted a beautiful picture of what the evening could be like. He would fix steaks on the grill, along with his specialty — a salad that he would toss with his own hands. They would spend the evening sipping a fine wine in front of a fireplace, holding hands, and discussing the Dewey Decimal System. These were not the plans that Skip actually had for the evening, but his story was good enough to get her to go with him.

In the meantime, his two roommates had spent the afternoon in a redneck bar, drinking and listening to Hank Williams, Jr., on the jukebox. They had picked up two old redneck girls and taken them back to the apartment. One girl was wearing a T-shirt that said, "Born to Wiggle." The other was wearing white cowgirl boots and a sequined tank top. The four of them built a roaring fire and opened a two-gallon wine jug and a twelve-pack of Miller High Life. They turned the stereo wide open and sat down in front of the fireplace to soak up some of the atmosphere they had created.

Meanwhile, our hero Skip is driving toward this scene of debauchery with his straight-laced librarian friend sitting a respectable distance from him. He couldn't wait to impress his classy companion with his posh new digs. They walked hand in hand to the front door, and he pushed it wide open so she could drink in its beauty and grandeur.

They were blasted in the face by the sounds of Jerry Lee Lewis destroying a piano and screaming, "Whole lotta shakin' goin' on." On the floor in front of the fireplace were four drunks surrounded by a low parapet of empty beer cans and full ashtrays. The place was a disaster area.

Skip never said a word. He just closed the door as his librarian friend ran crying into the cool Georgia night. So much for Skip's brief journey into respectability.

On a trip to Montreal to cover a Braves game, Skip once again met and fell in love with another beautiful Canadian girl. He found just enough time to pledge his undying love for her before he had to fly back to reality. He called her every day, and the long-distance love affair was going hot and heavy.

One night he called her after more than a few drinks. They talked, and he kept drinking. Midway through the conversation, he dozed off. She was so insulted that she never took his calls again. He lost both ways, because after he went to sleep, the telephone connection remained open, and his phone bill for that one call was $122.00 — no small amount in the early seventies.

There was also the time I had a very special guest on my radio show — Guenella Knutson. She was a real beauty and a former Miss Sweden. She had become world famous doing Noxzema shaving cream commercials. While a man was shaving, she would look in the camera and purr in her heavy Swedish accent, "Take it off . . . take it all off."

When Skip heard her on the radio, he came straight to the station, took me aside, and told me to fix him up with a dinner date with this international beauty. I told him I would try, and, surprisingly, she agreed to have dinner with him.

When I asked him the next day about the date, he said they had a nice Italian dinner at Cognito's, and since she had an early flight, she kissed him goodnight at the door and that was that. He described it as a nice evening, but uneventful.

Several years later, I was doing a late-night show, and once again Miss Knutson was my guest. Skip again hurried to the radio station to see her. Imagine his surprise when she failed to remember him or their date.

Maybe foreign women have trouble understanding Skip.

I have liked all of Skip's wives and most of his girlfriends, which, if nothing else, is a testimony to my own eclectic tastes. The girlfriends, in particular, are a diverse lot, ranging from beautiful, talented celebrities to bleach-blonde bubbleheads with the IQ of a carrot.

The Knights of Columbus asked me if I would help them raise some funds. They wanted me and Skip to make a joint speech. I thought it sounded like a fun thing to do. They would have two podiums on the stage; Skip would tell a story, then I would tell a story, and the money we raised would go to charity.

I called Skip and he said he would be glad to do it if I would have him out of there by nine o'clock. I asked why he had to leave so early. He said, "You know that old girl I've been dating? Well, she has promised to come home with me that night."

Skip had been dating a local celebrity, and she was an absolute beauty. Jokingly, I said, "I'll have you out by nine on one condition."

"What is it?"

"As soon as it's over, you have to call me and tell me."

It never occurred to me that he would take me seriously until my phone rang about 2:00 a.m.

"Hello," I mumbled.

"At 12:37 a.m., in front of a fireplace, on a bearskin rug . . ."

I stopped him: "Are you about to tell me what I think you are about to tell me?"

"You asked me to call," he said.

"I was kidding."

"You didn't smile," Skip said.

I know you must be wondering who the woman was. I have not used her name because you would recognize it and I would be either sued or beaten senseless.

If, however, you really want to know, call me and I'll tell you. The story's better when you know her name.

On another occasion, Skip and I planned a trip to the Sugar Bowl; I took my wife, and Skip took a young lady I'll call Buffy. I will call her Buffy in case anybody ever reads this to her. I wouldn't want to hurt her feelings. She was a junior in college and a striking beauty. She had jet black hair and the complexion of a porcelain doll. When you looked deeply into her eyes, however, it was like looking down an elevator shaft.

We were in our room watching a football game on TV, and I was trying to kick up a little conversation.

"When are you going to graduate?" I asked her.

"Next October or June or sometime like that," she answered.

"That's nice," I said, plodding onward. "What are you going to do when you graduate?"

"I'm going to be either a sportswriter or a sports reporter on television," she declared.

"Really? How exciting . . . you must really be a sports fan."

"Oh, I love all sports," she said.

"Well, I sure wish you luck." We both then returned our attention to the football game on TV.

"Can I ask you a question?" she said after a minute.

"Sure," I said.

"What are all those white lines on the field?"

I didn't want to laugh, and I didn't want her to feel stupid, so I went into some length to explain. When I finished explaining, she smiled and said, "Neat!"

I don't know what Buffy's doing today, but I sure hope she married well.

The
Second Time
Around

For awhile there, after the divorce from Nancy, it seemed to me Skip moved twice a month. It shouldn't have bothered me how often he moved, except for some reason, I always seemed to be in charge of the move. I would gather all my children and the friends of my children, and we would borrow pickup trucks and just have at it.

In one year, we moved Skip from Atlanta to Stone Mountain, from Stone Mountain to Decatur, and from Decatur to Atlanta. During these moves, Skip's roommate was Ron Jenkins. Skip and Ron are both top-seeded beer drinkers. They were both in their twenties, and neither one of them had ever in their whole lives thrown a beer can into a trash can. Wherever they finished a beer was where the can stayed. It was not uncommon at all for there to be two hundred beer cans scattered around whatever hovel they were living in at the moment. Before any move took place, it was necessary to take plastic garbage bags in and haul all the cans away. Next, you had to wash all the dishes. Then, and only then, could the actual move start.

Once, when we were packing, we discovered that Skip had over a hundred pairs of jockey shorts in a drawer. When I asked him why he needed a hundred pair of shorts, he explained, "Well, I don't wash clothes very often, and when I run short of clean underdrawers, I stop by Sears and buy a six-pack."

Obviously, it was time for Skip to settle down again.

Skip had been dating Fay for several months, and it was easy to see that he was falling more in love with her every day. I knew that someday she was going to become the second Mrs. Grizzard. However, for some time she was less than enthusiastic about standing before the altar with the Skipper. Every day he would ask her to marry him, and every day she would tell him no.

Fay had a beautiful singing voice and wanted to be in show business. She knew that marriage would not help her career, and she wanted her freedom to chase her dream. I knew she was right, but Skip was so much in love, there was just no way he was going to understand her ambition. And when he turned on that famous Grizzard charm, it was very difficult for anybody to refuse him anything.

Fay was not only a beautiful woman; she was a very good person. She laughed at all my stories, which made me just as much in favor of the marriage as Skip.

One afternoon about five-thirty, there was a knock on my door. When I opened it up, there stood Skip and the lovely Fay. Skip grabbed me around the neck with a big hug and said, "Fay said yes, and you have got to get us married tonight."

We all hugged and laughed and kissed. Finally, I said, "So when are y'all going to get married?"

"You ain't listening," Skip said. "We're going to get married tonight, and you're going to fix it so we can."

"Do you have your license?" I asked.

"License? No, we don't have a license. Can you get us one?"

"Have you had your blood test?" I asked.

"No. Can you fix it up?"

"It's almost six o'clock at night," I pointed out. "There is no way on God's earth you two can get married tonight."

Skip got real quiet, put both hands on my shoulders, looked me right in the eye, and rolled out about two yards of Grizzard smooth. "I love Fay more than I ever loved anybody," he declared in a reverential tone, "and I don't want the sun to rise again in the east without her being my wife."

I knew it was useless to argue, so I said, "Okay, let's get on the phone and try to find a marriage mill."

I had heard for years about places in Florida and North Georgia where the only things you needed to get married were ten minutes and fifty dollars. I started calling every town on my mental list, but they all said the same thing: "No way."

I called one town where the only place open was the local funeral home. The undertaker on duty said they could get married in one hour, but they would have to wait until City Hall opened up in the morning. I told him that the prospective groom had just escaped from the Viet Cong after being a POW for five years. Not only that, but he was a Congressional Medal of Honor winner, was a runner-up for the Nobel Peace Prize, and once tied for second place in a Ferlin Husky look-alike contest. The undertaker said that was impressive, but once City Hall closed for the night, they wouldn't open up if the Pope wanted to get married.

It was getting close to midnight when we decided that the wedding would have to wait until the next day. We made our plans. Bright and early the next morning, Skip and Fay would go get a marriage license and a blood test. My wife would get a cake, and I would find a preacher.

We called a few friends and told them to be there at six o'clock for the wedding. I called my minister and was told that he had just suffered a heart attack and was in the hospital. The assistant preacher was deep-sea fishing in Florida. I called every minister I knew, but for one reason or another, none of them was available.

I was starting to panic. I had talked to Skip on the phone; he had the license and, praise God, he had the blood test. Everything was a go, except for my part of the arrangement.

Suddenly I remembered a guy I had worked with in the insurance business. He was a full-time insurance man, but also did some gospel singing, played the piano, and was a part-time preacher. I called him at the insurance company where he worked, and he confirmed that he was a licensed minister.

"Can you marry people?" I asked.

"Well," he said slowly, "I never have, but I guess legally I can do it."

"Can you be at my house at six o'clock tonight?"

"I don't know," he hedged. "I really never married anybody before, and I'm not sure I know exactly how to do it."

"You must have a book somewhere with the marriage ceremony in it," I pointed out.

"I guess I do," he admitted, "but I don't know if I can do it to suit everybody."

"I'll give you fifty dollars."

"I'll be there at six o'clock," he said.

I called Skip and told him we had our preacher, and Skip immediately asked what denomination he was. I said, "I don't care if he's a Hindu; the point is he can marry you." He seemed satisfied.

"What do you want for a wedding present?" I asked him.

"We want to go to Florida on a train," Skip answered at once.

I told him that would be our wedding present. I would get them a private compartment on a Florida-bound train. I called Amtrak and was shocked to find that no passenger trains ran from Atlanta to the Sunshine State. The only train connection I could make was out of Savannah, and the train pulled out at about three in the morning. Skip said that would be wonderful. They would drive from my house after the wedding and be in Savannah in plenty of time to catch the train.

I went to Brookwood Station and picked up the tickets. I felt like the problems of the world had been lifted from my shoulders. When I got home, the house was all set for the Big Event. My wife had the cake, and there were flowers and balloons everywhere. It was a little gaudy, if anything, but, after all, it was short notice, and this was not an ordinary wedding. We had invited some close friends, and miracle of miracles, it was beginning to look like we had put together a very nice wedding in something under twenty-four hours.

It was decided that my preacher friend would not only perform the ceremony, but would play the organ and sing. Believe it or not, his first selection was "Why Me, Lord." To our credit, we all kept a straight face.

We stashed the bride in one bedroom, and Skip and I stayed in another bedroom. We were to wait there until time for the ceremony. We drank beer, and Skip was the happiest I had ever seen him. He was truly a man in love. When the time came, we went into the den and stood in our appointed places.

The preacher played the Wedding March, and the bride made her entrance. She was so lovely that the groom was smiling like he had just stolen a government check, but the preacher was an absolute wreck. I had never seen a human being so nervous. I remember thinking, "He is going to have a heart attack and die. We're going to have a dead preacher on our den floor, and they're still not going to be married."

We stood there in silence while he turned the pages in his book looking for the wedding ceremony. He kept turning pages, and turning pages, and, God please help him, turning pages. After what seemed like two weeks, my wife reached over and took the book from his trembling hands, found the right page, and handed it back. He took a deep breath and started with, "It says here, 'Dearly Beloved, we are gathered here . . .' "

That's about all I remember hearing. I was busy watching him to see if I could detect any sign of chest pain reflected in his face. God was good to us; the next thing I remember him saying was, "You may now kiss the bride." We all hugged and kissed the bride and lied to each other about what a beautiful ceremony it was. We ate ice cream and cake, drank champagne, and had a nice, brief wedding reception.

When it was time for their departure, we walked them to their car through a shower of rice and hugged and kissed some more. I took out the Amtrak tickets and put them in Skip's inside coat pocket. I explained to him that the car number and compartment number were written on the envelope containing the tickets. Skip was excited as a puppy, and I could tell he was only half-listening.

When they drove out of my driveway, the only person more relieved than I was my friend the preacher. We said goodbye to our guests, cleaned up the den, and finally fell into bed exhausted. I'm not sure what time the phone rang, but it must have been somewhere around 3:00 a.m.

Skip was screaming into the phone, absolutely furious. "I'm surprised at you," he yelled, "pulling a trick like this."

"What are you talking about?" I asked.

"I knew you were big on practical jokes," he stormed on, "but I can't believe you would pull a stunt like this."

I asked him again to calm down and tell me what he was talking about.

"You know damn well what I'm talking about. The people at Amtrak have never heard of me. They don't have any reservation for me, and they don't have any compartments available. We're going to have to spend our wedding night sitting in a train car full of people, and it's all your fault."

"Show them your tickets," I suggested. "They have the car and compartment number written on them."

"Tickets? What tickets?" Skip demanded. "You didn't give me any tickets."

"Look in your inside coat pocket," I told him.

"There are no tickets there," he hollered. "You have ruined my wedding night. You have ruined my life." He went on and on: "You think this is a joke. Well, let me tell you one thing . . . this is not funny!"

"Skip," I said, "you're absolutely right. This is not funny, but let me tell you something that is funny. Do you remember the man who married you, the one you *thought* was a preacher?" The phone went silent as I went on: "Well, he is actually a friend of mine who works at the American Oil Station up on the Roosevelt Highway, and that, Skip, *is* funny." Before he could speak, I hung up the phone.

I don't know what he told Fay, but I do know that he went on his honeymoon not knowing if he was married or not.

He was, of course, but not for very long. Because if there have been one or two things in Skip's life that have worked out like he planned them, marriage is certainly not one of them. Still, we had some good times during the Fay years, including one memorable trip to Louisville, Kentucky. I have to preface this story, however, by pointing out that Skip Grizzard is probably the most competitive person I have ever known. He likes to win and is willing to put out whatever effort is necessary to make sure he comes out a winner.

In his sportswriting days, he was always the last person to leave the press box. I never saw him come out of that box until every other writer had been gone for at least two hours. He refused to turn his story in until he was absolutely sure it was his best work.

We both enjoy playing cards and have probably been in ten thousand card games together. He is a good sport when he loses, but you can see in his face that he will not be satisfied until you play one more game and he has erased that loss from the scorekeeping part of his brain.

We played softball on the same team for two or three years. He played every pitch like it was the seventh game of the World Series. In one game that didn't mean a thing, he made a head-first slide into second that was so jarring it broke his glasses in half.

To go to a University of Georgia football game with him is a great experience. He not only cheers himself hoarse; he gives you a running account of his philosophy throughout the game. If Georgia is playing a team from outside the South, he will say things like, "This is much, much more than a mere college football game. What this actually is is our way of life against their way of life." If Georgia's opponent is from outside Georgia, he will say things like, "These people have no history; no tradition. I don't know much, but I do know that God wants us to beat these people." And if Georgia's opponent is Georgia Tech, well, Skip is simply beside himself. If UGA should be tied, or God forbid, behind at the half, he is literally sick with worry.

In his tennis playing days, every game was Wimbledon. Anytime he had a racket in his hand, he was wide open, teeth clenched, and had the world's most determined look on his face. He was in Chicago for three years and never missed a day playing tennis. He located an indoor tennis facility before he located an apartment.

In the last few years he has attacked golf with the same spirit that he applies to the rest of his life. If the weather is nice and I cannot locate Skip on the golf course, I start checking the hospitals and the morgue. Nothing, and I mean absolutely nothing, can keep him off the links. Not many people enjoy *anything* like he enjoys golf.

To get back to the story, we decided one year that we were going to ride a train to Louisville, Kentucky, and see the Kentucky Derby. We both like trains, and we figured this would be the trip of a lifetime. Fay's parents lived in Louisville, so it would be a nice homecoming for her as well. We rode a train to Birmingham, changed trains there, and went on to Kentucky. We were wined and dined and went to every derby party in town. We had enough mint juleps to fill a tank car. I hate to admit it, but the truth is we got so busy going to derby parties that we forgot to go to the race.

During an afternoon at Fay's parents' house, somebody suggested that we get up a volleyball game. I'm not sure if it was the joy of the competition or the mint juleps, but Skip was so happy he almost wet his pants. The volleyball net was quickly strung up in the backyard, and immediately we heard Skip shout, "Let the games begin!" We decided that since this was just going to be a friendly, family volleyball game, everybody would play, even the small children. After all, it was all in fun.

Fay's little sister was almost five years old at the time. She was a beautiful child, barely three feet tall, with blonde curly hair. She was wearing a red dress and had on little black patent leather shoes with white socks rolled down one roll. She was precious.

She asked if she could join in the game. We knew that she was too small to do anything but get in the way, but how do you say no to a child that tiny and adorable?

Everybody was having fun, and nobody seemed to be taking the game too seriously. Nobody, that is, except Skip. He was yelling out the score and cheering on his team like some kind of Southern Knute Rockne.

He was playing on the back line when a ball was hit high above the net. He charged like an enraged rhino, leapt like a gazelle, and with a closed fist smashed the ball downward with all his might. The ball hit the little girl right between the eyes. She went down like a sack of potatoes, bawling her lungs out. Luckily she wasn't hurt badly, but I took Skip aside and said, "Are you crazy? You could have hurt that child."

"I thought she was trying to score," Skip said.

I don't know if Skip's clobbering Fay's little sister had anything to do with the eventual breakup, but it probably didn't help the marriage.

Major
Talent

Skip Grizzard is a very talented man. He is a gifted writer, one of the finest public speakers in America, and a trivia player of some renown. He also has a talent that most people do not give him credit for. He is, without any doubt, the most creative liar to women ever to walk on the planet earth. He can tell a woman that he finished third in last year's Kentucky Derby, and she will go right out and buy him a saddle.

The person upon whom he first practiced his craft was, of course, his mother. Skip had, without a doubt, one of the most loving, understanding mothers that ever lived. Miss Christine was a schoolteacher, and just as Southern as sweet iced tea. She had such a kind, gentle heart that I don't think she could realize most people did not share her goodness. She loved Skip as only a mother could; I'm convinced that, in her mind, the Skipper could do no wrong.

One night, when Skip was about sixteen, he came home after a long evening of Pabst Blue Ribbon. It was late, and everybody in the house was in bed and long since asleep. Skip decided he was hungry, and, like any hungry sixteen-year-old, he headed for the refrigerator. He was careful to make no noise, so as not to bring anyone into the kitchen to notice his drunken condition. He spotted a large bowl of Miss Christine's famous potato salad in the very back of the bottom shelf and got down on his knees for a better reach. His mind was heavily fogged by the Pabst Blue Ribbon, and the cool air rushing out of the refrigerator felt good. He put his head inside and realized that the cool air made him feel much better. In fact, he was so enjoying the cool that he forgot he was hungry.

"This is great," he thought. "Suddenly, right here in Moreland, Georgia, I am on the slopes at Aspen skiing downhill and having the time of my life." He rested his head on the bottom shelf and decided he would stay there for just a minute or two—it felt so good. There he was in the kitchen, on his knees, with his head stuck in the refrigerator, and before he knew it, he was sound asleep.

It's hard to believe that anyone could sleep in that position, but with enough Pabst Blue Ribbon under your belt, I guess you could sleep in a wheelbarrow.

When the sun came up over Coweta County, Skip was still there sound asleep. Miss Christine came in the kitchen shortly after sunup to fix breakfast and found him there on the floor. She shook Skip awake and in her soft Southern drawl asked the question that only a loving mother would ask: "Skipper, have you been drinking?"

No, Skip told her; it was just too hot to sleep in his bedroom. It was a story only a mother could buy.

Many years later, we were going to see the University of Georgia play Tulane in New Orleans. I was taking my wife, and Skip was taking the young lady he had been dating. We had been planning our trip for weeks, and at the last minute Skip called to say that he had a problem and didn't know how to handle it. He said that he had been badly overserved by a local bartender, and while in the clutches of Jack Daniels he had invited another woman to go with us to the game. As the story unfolded, it turned out that he had invited two other women to go.

I said, "Well, it sounds like you're going to have a fun weekend, but don't you think the car is going to be a little crowded?"

It turned out okay. The *Journal* had started using color pictures in the sports section, so Skip told one of the women he had to go to Dallas to a color seminar. He told the other one that his little brother, Joey, had been kicked in the head by a mule and was in a coma. Both women believed him, and we drove down south with Skip singing "The City of New Orleans" at the top of his lungs.

On another occasion, Diane and I had joined Skip and his lovely young companion at a restaurant. When the waiter brought the wine, Skip said he wanted to propose a toast. He raised his glass and, turning to his date, said, "To the next Mrs. Grizzard."

That was not the first—or last—time Diane and I heard that toast, but we didn't hesitate to wish them much happiness. We had some more wine, and Skip was really getting into the spirit of the evening. He said, "I can see it now—after we get settled in our new house, we'll invite y'all over for dinner. It'll be a white house with one of those picket fences all around the yard. We'll have cedar yard furniture under a big shade tree in the back yard. While the women are in the house frying the chicken and making the mashed potatoes, we'll sit under that big old tree and play with our puppy. After dinner, we'll sit around, drink a little wine, and hold hands with the two most beautiful women in the state of Georgia." He went on for ten more minutes painting this beautiful picture about spending the rest of his life in wedded bliss.

When he took a breath, his date excused herself to go to the ladies room. She was barely out of earshot when he turned to me and said, "Ain't no way on God's green earth I'll ever marry her."

My favorite lie was one that took all of Skip's charm and imagination. He had told me over and over how much he loved Fay, and it was true; when he was around her it showed. They had made plans to meet at his apartment at seven o'clock to go to dinner. About two o'clock, some other woman called him, and he asked her to come over. As Skip said later, she delivered.

They had a drink or two, and as the afternoon wore on, they followed their inclinations and wound up in bed. It was a small apartment, and the bed was right next to double French doors that led to a patio.

At some point during the latter part of the afternoon, there was a knock at the front door.

"Who is it?" Skip called out.

"It's Fay. Let me in. I got off early."

"I can't right now," Skip said.

"Skip, open this door!" Fay demanded.

"I'll call you," he said, and heard her walk away. He whispered to the woman in bed with him, "Be quiet . . . I think she's leaving."

At that instant he heard Fay's footsteps on the patio and realized, to his horror, that the French doors were not locked. He jumped up and grabbed the door handle just as it was opening, and a tug-of-war commenced.

"Skip," Fay exclaimed, "have you lost your mind? Let me in!"

"I can't let you in," Skip mumbled. "I don't have any clothes on."

"Well, I won't look then. Just turn the door loose."

Now in blind panic, Skip could only come up with, "I'll call you and we'll have a nice dinner later. Go home and I'll call you."

"Don't bother!" Fay hissed through clenched teeth, then stomped off the patio.

Skip called me and told me the whole story. He was really worried and didn't know what to do. The only advice I had was, the sooner he called her, the better it would be. He said he would call her as soon as he could come up with a story, and I told him to call me back and let me know what happened. I was concerned, too. I knew that Skip really did love Fay, and it looked like this might be the end of the line.

In about an hour Skip called to say everything was all right. "Do you all want to meet us somewhere for dinner?" he asked.

I was amazed. He had gone from being almost suicidal with worry to the most cheerful man in America in a matter of minutes. "What happened?" I asked. "What did you tell her?"

According to his report, the conversation went like this:

Skip: "Hi, Sugar. How ya doing?"
Fay: "Fine!"
Skip: "Were you over a little earlier?"
Fay: "What?! You know full well . . ."

Skip (interrupting): "I was taking a nap, and I had the dangdest dream. I dreamed that there was a mad dog out in the parking lot of my apartment. He was foaming at the mouth and growling. He was a great big old dog."

Fay: "What's that got to do . . ."

Skip (interrupting again): "My neighbors were trying to get me to come out so the dog could bite me, but I wouldn't go. Finally they got you to try to get me to come out. I was too afraid to come out even for you. It was the worst nightmare I ever had. When I woke up, I was soaking wet with sweat."

Fay: "You know, Skip, that's exactly what happend! I'll tell you all about it when I get there."

The man is beautiful.

In addition to the wonderfully creative individual lies that he's come up with over the years, he also used to have what I call his "stock" lie. He was the executive sports editor of the paper at the time, and he used this lie anytime he was being pressed by a woman to go someplace he didn't want to go or spend more time with her than he wanted to spend. The stock lie goes like this:

"You know I love you, and you know that if I had my way I would be with you more, but it's a real zoo at the paper right now. But as soon as _____ season (fill in the blank with the appropriate sport—football, baseball, or basketball) is over, we're going to take a wonderful trip to the mountains. We'll take moonlight walks in the woods. We'll drink fine wine in front of a crackling fire. I'll fix steaks on a grill, and we'll spend hours in a hot-tub. No phones, no newspapers . . . just the two of us and the mountains."

Needless to say, the stock lie got him off the hook every time.

In the years before his name and face were well known, he had some great opening lies that he used on women he just met in bars. They included, but were not limited to:

- "You're beautiful. How would you like to be a TV weather girl?"
- "What a coincidence . . . my mother's name was Winotte Rose, too."
- "I know you've heard this before, but you really look like Kim Novak."
- "What a nice voice you have. What radio station do you work at?"
- "May I have your autograph, Miss Lolabrigida?"
- "Haven't I seen you on TV?"
- "I never believed in love at first sight till this very minute."
- "If Bette had your eyes, she would still be a star."

● "I'm from Vegas. Have you ever been on a Lear jet?"

● "You remind me of my mother" (an oldie, but a goodie).

Skip had been keeping steady company with a lovely young lady who was a very recent graduate of Auburn University. They went everywhere together, up to and including several trips to Europe. He bought her beautiful gifts, and almost everyone in their circle of friends thought that perhaps, just perhaps, she would be the next Mrs. Grizzard. I knew better. The only thing she had going for her was a pretty face and a sweet disposition.

There was nothing between them that indicated to me she was anything more to Skip than a good companion. Then, inevitably, the relationship reached the point where Skip was never without her, and I could see it was beginning to cramp his style.

He called her one day and faked being in a deep depression. He told her that his publisher had just called him from New York and had really raked him over the coals because his book was not in on time. He told her that they had threatened not to publish his book if they did not have the completed manuscript in their office in ten days. He went on to say that he had no choice but to check into a hotel, lock himself in the room, take no phone calls, eat in his room, and not go out until the book was finished. That way, he might be able to get the book in on time and avoid being blackballed by the publishers of the world.

She asked the obvious question: "What hotel are you going to?"

Skip said he had not decided, but would call her and let her know. She told him not to work too hard and to call her as soon as he could. He assured her he would.

He hung up the phone, got into his car, picked up another young lady at her house, went to the airport and flew to Colorado for a week of skiing and God knows what.

If the Auburn graduate ever suspected anything, she didn't mention it.

It may not be lying, exactly, but Skip also has a way of leading his lady friends to believe that they are engaged to him. You know how an engagement is supposed to happen: The young man gets down on one knee, professes his love in long, flowery phrases, produces an engagement ring, and asks the young lady in question if she will walk hand in hand with him down the highways and by-ways of life. He then goes to the father of the damsel, again professes his great love, and asks for the daughter's hand in marriage. The father says yes, the mother bawls, "My baby, my baby!" and everybody hugs. The engagement announcement is put in the local paper, and on the day the paper comes out, the happy couple is officially engaged.

It works a little differently with Skip's engagements. The last time he got down on one knee, he was trying to line up a 25-foot putt. I'm not at all sure that he has ever used the phrase, "Will you marry me?" I am not sure (and neither is Skip) how many times he has gone with a woman who considered herself engaged to him.

Most of his engagements took place in one of two ways. Either he was simply drinking too much and asked the woman to marry him, or else he was dating the woman and she caught him fooling around with somebody else. In this second scenario, the alleged proposal would be Skip's attempt to escape the woman's fury over his infidelity. Skip has no stomach, whatsoever, for a woman's wrath. He would much rather be in the room with an enraged leopard than with what he calls a "quarrelsome woman." In the midst of such a tongue-lashing, he would agree to anything that would smooth the waters. When I would ask later, "Skip, are you really engaged to her?" he would drop his eyes and mumble, "Well, I guess we're kinda engaged."

"What does 'kinda engaged' mean?" I would ask.

He would smile and say, "Well, that means that she is more engaged than I am."

I have absolutely lost count of the times he has been "kinda engaged."

His most unlikely "kinda" fiancée was a very attractive young lady whom I will call Pat. I don't know how they got to be "kinda engaged"; they had almost nothing in common. She was a devout Christian, while Skip thought Sampson and the Philistines were a rock group. She was a faithful member of the Baptist Tabernacle, and he had never been inside. In addition, she had two small children, not an asset with Skip. She didn't drink or smoke and seemed very uncomfortable when she was around people having a cocktail. Apparently, the only thing they had in common was an interest in sex.

In those days, Skip had a standard way of breaking off his "kinda engagements." His M.O. was to avoid his "kinda fiancée" and at the same time become more flagrant in his womanizing. He figured if she caught him or even suspected he was fooling around, her pride would cause her to break off the engagement without too much bloodletting. Sometimes it worked; sometimes it didn't. With Pat, it didn't. She seemed to think that it was her Christian duty to overlook his drinking, cussing, smoking, and womanizing, and, by some miracle, to bring him to the foot of the cross.

I was at his apartment one night when, despite all his efforts, she was still calling him. He was so frustrated by her refusal to leave him alone and go the way of so many other fiancées that he lost his temper and started to curse: "Damn it, Pat, I've told you to leave me the f--- alone. We don't have a g-d--- thing in common. Don't call me anymore. I'm tired of your nagging b---s---!" With that, he screamed "GOODBYE!" and slammed the receiver down into the cradle. He turned to me and said, "She's crazy, really out of her mind, nuts!"

The phone rang, and, still angry, he shouted, "Hello!" Pat said, "Have you decided to accept Jesus Christ as your personal savior?" He slammed the receiver down again.

Pat was a strange young lady. I really believe she was a sincere, dedicated Christian. I know what attracted Skip to Pat, but I have never been quite sure what attracted her to him. Perhaps it was the challenge.

I don't mean to imply that Skip always lies to women. It's just that lying seems to work better than telling the truth does.

One night Skip was enjoying dinner and twelve or fourteen drinks at Joe Dale's Cajun House Restaurant. As usual, he was in the company of a very lovely, slightly-past-teenage young lady. He had already started his campaign to make sure he would have the pleasure of her company until at least the first commercial break on the "Today" show. He was being as smooth as David Niven, but the young lady kept assuring him that she had no interest in seeing his apartment, or the Bible he kept there that once belonged to his great-great-grandfather, General Stonewall R. Grizzard. In short, Skip was striking out.

The situation even got worse when he said, "Do you mind if I smoke?" and she replied, "I don't care if you burst into flames."

After another drink and more small talk, she announced that she was going to the ladies' room. Ever the gentleman, Skip volunteered to walk with her. On the way, they passed a large picture of yours truly that my friend Joe Dale had displayed there. Skip stopped and said, "There's a picture of my brother."

"Get out of here," the young lady replied. "That's Ludlow Porch."

"I know," Skip said. "Ludlow's my brother."

"Sure, sure," said the skeptical young woman, "and your great-great-grandfather was called Stonewall."

"Okay," Skip declared. "I'll prove it to you. I'll call him and let you talk."

It was almost two in the morning, and I was sound asleep when the phone woke me up. I answered and heard this cheery voice say, "Big Lud, this is the Skipper. Did I wake you up?"

"It's the middle of the night. Of course you woke me up."

"Listen," he said, "my date and I are at Joe Dale's, and we saw your picture and she doesn't believe we're brothers."

"She doesn't?" I answered. "Let me talk to her."

Then I heard this slightly embarrassed voice ask, "Is this Ludlow Porch?"

"Lady," I said, "I don't know who you and that other drunk are, but you've got your nerve calling decent people in the middle of the night." Then I slammed the phone down.

I can only assume that the Skipper slept alone that night.

Aero, Medico, and other Phobias

When I tell you that Skip was afraid to fly, what I really mean is that he was terrified to fly. I'm not sure exactly where this fear came from, but I know that for many years, there was no way to get him on an airplane. In today's business world, refusing to fly makes life very difficult.

I decided that if I could get four or five drinks into him, we could overcome his phobia. He was going somewhere or other to cover a football game, and I was able to persuade him that contrary to what the experts said, it was possible to find courage when you were arm and arm with Jack Daniels. My wife and I took him to the airport and got there early enough for a visit to the Crown Room. I made sure that his glass was full for ninety minutes, and he got braver and braver with every drink. By the time we got him to his gate, he was telling us about his secret ambition to be a wing walker and barnstorm the country.

The last thing he said was, "This is going to be a piece of cake. I'm going to volunteer for the Flying Tigers as soon as I get back." He disappeared down the tunnel, softly humming, "Off We Go, into the Wild Blue Yonder," and I felt like the world's greatest psychiatrist.

On the way home, we stopped for a nice, leisurely dinner. When we drove into our driveway a few hours later, there was Skip sitting on his suitcase waiting for us.

"How far did you get?" I asked.

"By the time I got to the first class section I was completely sober," he said, "and I knew that all the people around me were going to die in a fiery crash."

Once, when he was the sports editor for the Chicago *Sun Times*, he got a job offer from a newspaper in San Francisco. They wanted him to fly out for an interview. It was a great opportunity, so rather than fly, he took two weeks vacation and rode a train all the way to San Francisco. He simply planned his life so that he never had to face the stark terror of getting on another airplane. He made a lot of jokes about it, but Skip's fear of flying was absolutely paralyzing.

In 1977, my mother died, and Skip was still living in Chicago. Someone called him and told him what had happened. I want you to know that he caught the next plane to Atlanta.

Flying, however, is only one of the fears that Skip carries with him. One night we both wound up at what was billed as a seance. It was held in the private home of a friend of ours who believed in such things. There were ten or twelve people there, and our hostess had set up a nice bar in the kitchen.

When the seance started, we were told that the spirits would not come if there were any light except candlelight. So the electric lights were turned off, and four women sat down around a card table and held hands. With the candles flickering and our hostess speaking to the spirits, it looked like a scene out of an old Basil Rathbone movie. Except for the three candles burning in the living room, the whole apartment was dark, including the kitchen where the bar was set up.

"I want a drink," Skip whispered in my ear.

"The bar is in the kitchen," I said. "Help yourself."

"It's dark in there," he said.

"So take a candle with you."

"Will you go with me?"

I'm afraid I disturbed the approaching spirits with my outburst of laughter. I couldn't believe it. He was actually afraid to go into that dark kitchen alone. We never did contact any ghosts, but that was the biggest laugh I had had in years.

Skip is probably the only person in the history of medical science to make more money off his heart surgery than his doctor. He has made dozens of speeches about it and written hundreds of newspaper columns recounting his near meeting with St. Peter.

He even wrote a book about it called *They Tore Out My Heart and Stomped That Sucker Flat*. In whatever medium, he has managed to find a lot of humor in what could easily have been his last time at bat.

He will tell anybody who will listen that the doctors and nurses at Emory University Hospital saved his life, but that's now. He had a different attitude beforehand.

On the morning of his first surgery, I was alone with him in his room. His worst nightmare was about to come true. Someone he hardly knew was going to cut him with a knife, and he was not going to be able to hotfoot it out of the area. Like anybody, Skip was scared to death. I was making small talk, trying not to be morbid, when suddenly he reached up and took my hand. It was to me a very tender, moving moment. In a voice barely above a whisper he said, "Lud, you have to promise me something."

"Anything, anything," I said, practically sobbing.

He swallowed and said, "If I should die, kill the doctor."

There's a curious disease that nobody has ever found a cure for. It's called Black Cord Fever, and it afflicts males with a particular predisposition: those who are both a) drinking and b) afraid to be alone.

Lewis and Skip both suffered from Black Cord Fever. It is not a fatal disease, but it can be expensive. When you are infected, you pour yourself another drink, find the nearest telephone, and call everybody you ever met in your life.

The first call is usually to a friend who is in your local dialing area. As the evening wears on, however, you start in on the long distance calls. It is not uncommon for a man with a bad case of Black Cord Fever to call the long distance operator to get the phone number of an old Army buddy in Syracuse whose last name he just can't remember.

I hope someday Jerry Lewis or somebody will put on a telethon for the victims of Black Cord Fever. Others may not see it as so important, but I have great sympathy for those who suffer from this malady because of my relationship with Lewis and Skip, both of whom should be poster adults for Black Cord Fever.

Skip called me at home one night. I knew at once that he was with Jack Daniels. He had worked all day at the Atlanta paper and had gone straight to a watering hole. It was about eleven o'clock, and he was pretty far along.

"Skip, where are you?" I asked.

He said, "If I tell you, you'll want to come get me."

I finally convinced him I wanted to meet him for a drink. He liked that idea and said he was at the downtown Marriott Hotel. I told him I would meet him in the lobby and that, no matter what happened, he was not to leave. He said he couldn't leave because he didn't remember where he had left his car.

I dressed quickly and went straight to the hotel lobby. No Skip. I went into the bar. Still no Skip. I checked the restaurant; he was nowhere to be found.

I was about ready to give up and call it a night when I noticed a phone booth in the lobby with the door closed and the receiver cradle empty. I walked over and peered in, and there sat the Skipper on the phone booth floor talking to a college buddy that he had not spoken to in years. He was wearing slacks and a white dress shirt, but had no recollection of where his coat, tie, or car was. He did, however, remember that we were going to have a drink together.

I convinced him to go home with me and we would try to find his car the next day. It took us all Saturday morning, but we finally found it in the parking lot of the old Mouse Trap Restaurant. We never did find his coat and tie.

Once, when Skip was living in Chicago, he called me. I knew the second I heard his voice that he had a bad case of Black Cord Fever. He was as homesick as any man could be; he was also very depressed. He and Fay were having problems, and she had moved out. He was so down that I was really worried about him. I tried to talk him into taking a few days off and flying home. He reminded me that he didn't fly. We talked for about an hour, and the longer we talked the more depressed he became. I finally said, "Skip, I'm coming after you." I hung up the phone and told my wife that we were driving to Chicago. If you don't know, Atlanta is about 45,000 miles from Chicago.

We got to the outskirts of the Windy City during their five o'clock rush. I stopped at a pay phone and called Skip for directions. He was so excited to hear a voice from home that he almost jumped through the phone. He gave me directions and said he would meet me at a certain intersection. I told him that the traffic was terrible, so he needed to allow me enough time to make it. We started into town in the worst traffic jam I had seen in years. When I was within a mile or so of our meeting spot, I saw Skip running down the center line of the four-lane street we were on. The traffic was just inching along, and he was looking in all the cars trying to find me.

When he finally got to our car, he laughed like a loon, and we must have hugged for ten minutes right there in the middle of the street. It was probably the finest reunion I was ever involved in.

Skip had made arrangements to go home with us for a few days, so we left Chicago and started south. It was during the C.B. radio craze, and Skip had watched carefully as I used the C.B. to get traffic and Smokey reports. We decided to drive all night so we could get Skip into the South before he absolutely busted a gut. I got sleepy, and Skip offered to drive while I caught a nap. We were cruising along about three in the morning, and as soon as I shut my eyes, Black Cord Fever hit Skip. He was lonely and just had to talk to somebody. There was the C.B. radio, and while he was not exactly sure how to use the thing, he just had to try. I was anxious to hear what he was going to say, so I didn't let on that I was still awake. He put the microphone to his mouth, and somewhere in the dark Indiana night I heard him say softly, "Hi there . . . my name is Skip Grizzard."

History does not tell us how many truckers laughed so hard they ran off the road.

Now that I think about it, it just may be that Skip's endless pursuit of women is not so much a result of his attraction to the opposite sex as of his fear of sleeping alone. In fact, on those evenings when he doesn't have the company of a lady friend, Skip sleeps with a black Lab named Catfish

Smith. The dog was a gift from Vince Dooley and was named for the legendary University of Georgia football player.

Catfish is a loving, delightful dog who manages to stay in trouble most of the time.

The following is a partial list of the things Catfish ate during the first year of his life:

2 TV remote controls;

2 pairs of eyeglasses;

2 eyeglass cases;

1 coffee table;

3 bannister railings;

1 banister;

1 complete set of patio furniture;

7 assorted dog bowls;

2 whole chickens;

1 bag of Reese's Peanut Butter Cups including all packaging;

1 leather wallet including Visa, Master-Card, and American Express cards;

1 sofa leg;

2 full-grown geese; and

1 set of car keys;

He was also the prime suspect in the disappearance of numerous other missing objects, but the items listed above have been proven to be his responsibility.

Whenever Skip was home alone with Catfish, he was constantly going to the door to let the dog out. Catfish loved the outdoors, and when he wanted to go out, he would bark nonstop until Skip responded.

Skip got the idea that his life would be greatly improved if he had a doggie door installed for the exclusive use of Mr. Catfish. The door was accordingly installed, Skip was off the hook, and Catfish was delighted.

Skip had to make an overnight trip and decided to leave the doggie door open so his dog could come and go as he pleased. He put out plenty food and water on the floor and departed on his journey.

He returned the next afternoon to find eleven dogs in his den. A large English Sheepdog was sound asleep on his sofa. There were dogs sleeping in chairs in front of his fireplace, and none of the visitors bothered to move or even wake up.

It was apparent that Catfish, like his master, did not like to sleep alone.

Proving
Murphy's
Law

Skip is one of the most gifted men I know. He writes three newspaper columns a week, each one better than the last. I have lost count of the number of books he has written, but I do know that people stand in line for hours to get him to autograph them. He is in demand all over the country as a speaker, and his comedy tapes sell like they were gold.

In recent months, he has started to test the waters as a country-western singer and songwriter. He is a better than average poker player and is one of the few people I know who can name all fifty state capitals. He knows all there is to know about railroads and has committed to memory coast-to-coast and border-to-border train schedules. He can tell you what time the Southern Crescent leaves Atlanta, what time it arrives in New Orleans, and all of the stops in between. He is a big-league trivia player and can quote batting averages from the National League all the way to the old Georgia-Florida league. He knows the name of every bartender in seven states.

Yet, with all his God-given talents, Skip is completely unequipped to live in the twentieth century. He could no more change a flat tire on his car than he could do brain surgery. His VCR has been blinking twelve o'clock at him for four years. His electric can opener has gone unused since Jimmy Carter was in the White House. Sometimes it seems that everything he touches turns to fatback.

Furthermore, Skip courts disaster every time he draws a breath. If something can go wrong, it will. In the 1960s, he was the slot man at the *Journal-Constitution*. It's an awful job, and while everybody else is out covering sporting events, drinking whiskey, and chasing women, the slot man is stuck at the paper, drawing lines on huge pieces of paper and fighting with the union types in the paper's composing room. In addition, the hours are long, the pay short, and no chance to get on the expense account. Skip worked for Jim Minter and Furman Bisher and was afraid of both of them. It was absolutely necessary that the slot man be at his desk not one second later than 6:00 a.m. To be late meant to face the wrath of both Bisher and Minter.

One night after work, Skip and two of his rowdy colleagues decided to go to Underground Atlanta for a few drinks before going home. They stayed until every seller of spiritous alcohol in Underground closed. But they had only been there about four or five hours, so they were, of course, still thirsty. There were not many after-hours spots in Atlanta at the time, so they decided to go clear across town to the Rodeway Inn, where the lounge stayed open until two o'clock. The Rodeway was next door to the Veteran's

Administration hospital, and when they arrived, they found several nurses there having an after-work drink. The sight of the attractive young nurses made Skip forget that he was tired from working all day. The only thing he knew was that there were women in the establishment and he, therefore, was on duty. It didn't take long to make the acquaintance of a young lady, and within an hour he had rented a room for the two of them. Nature took its course, and Skip was soon sleeping like a drunken baby.

The next time he looked at his watch, it was 5:30 a.m. He sprang out of bed like it was on fire. Thirty minutes to get to work. No time for a shower . . . no time for anything. He was all the way across town from the paper, and the clock was ticking. It suddenly hit him that he had left his car at the paper and the friend who had brought him was God knows where. He quickly called a taxi and told the dispatcher that it was life or death. When he walked out to the street to wait for his taxi, it was twenty-five minutes to six. He thought to check how much money he had left, and he almost cried when he found he only had a dollar and seventy-five cents. Where could all my money have gone? Then he remembered the drinks in Underground, and the lounge, and, of course, the cost of the room. He knew that the taxi fare would be much more than he had.

He was just seconds away from a complete nervous collapse when the taxi pulled up. He quickly explained his plight to the most unsympathetic cab driver in the greater Atlanta area. "Look, fella," the driver snarled, "if you were looking for charity, you should have called the Salvation Army. There ain't no way on earth that I can get you even close to the *Journal-Constitution* for a buck seventy-five."

Skip promised to mail him the money, send him four Superbowl tickets, and wax his cab if he would just drive him to the paper. Nothing seemed to sway him. He wanted his money then, and no amount of begging and pleading was going to change his mind.

"Okay," Skip finally decided, "take me into town a dollar seventy-five's worth."

With the clock ticking and the meter running, they started into town. When they were about two and a half miles from the paper, the cab driver pulled to the curb and said, "Okay, Mr. Rockerfeller, here we are. That'll be $1.75."

Skip pressed the money into his hand, got out of the car, and started to run south on Peachtree Street. He was dirty, unshaven, hung over, and sprinting down Peachtree Street with his head pounding harder at every step. But give him credit—he was at his desk at six o'clock.

On another occasion, while at the old Bucket Shop in Underground Atlanta for a round of after-work cocktails, Skip met and fell in love with a young lady. They had a few drinks and ate Bucket Burgers.

When it was time for the "your place or mine" question, the young lady suggested her place. Skip noticed that she did not live in a particularly good area, but by this time of the evening, he was blinded by his passion and would have cheerfully driven her to Maine had it been necessary. Besides, he had the next day off and could sleep late if he wanted to.

They proceeded to her place for the night, and when Skip woke up the next morning, he noticed that through some evil spell the young lady beside him had gotten ugly overnight. He slowly and silently got out of bed and, since he hated goodbyes, tried not to wake this former beauty snoring loudly beside him. He was not sure exactly where he was, but remembered that his car was outside the love nest. As he pulled on his clothes, he decided that he would stop for a Country Boy Breakfast at the Dunk-N-Dine, then go home, take a shower, lie around all day, and really get some rest on his day off. He closed the door silently behind him and tiptoed down the stairs. He was thinking, "I'm pretty sure I parked right in front of this apartment." Sure enough, there was his car, right where he had left it. As he got closer to the car, he couldn't help whistling, "Oh, what a beautiful morning."

When he got to the part about "a bright golden haze on the meadow," he froze. There was his dreamboat sitting neatly on concrete blocks with all four tires and all four wheels missing. His day had been ruined before it even started.

It's not only big things like VCRs, taxis, and stolen tires that conspire against Skip. There are also the little annoyances that seem to crop up every day of his life. I can assure you that he has lost his glasses every day for the past twenty-five years. I really believe that he could lose his glasses in a phone booth. You would think that a man who was blind as a hammer handle would try to have at least two pairs of glasses. Not Skip. He owns one pair at a time and loses them just about every twenty minutes.

He also locks his keys in his car on a regular basis. When that happens, he is absolutely helpless. He has no earthly idea how to go about retrieving them. On one occasion, he called his friend Ron Jenkins to come all the way from work in Decatur to downtown Atlanta to help get him back into his car. His last word to Ron was, "Oh yeah, better bring a coat hanger." When Ron got there with his coat hanger, he made Skip watch him open the car so he would know how to do it. Ron finished and said, "See how simple that is?" Skip said, "Oh, I would never be able to do all that. Come on . . . I'll buy you a beer."

Skip's life has been full of many victories, but the little defeats are never far behind. Several years ago he went to Colorado to learn how to ski. By all accounts, he was not a very good skier, but he really loved it. He bought enough clothes and gear for a family of Swedes. When he returned to Atlanta, he was really sold on winter sports in general and skiing in particular.

He was dating a young, very recent graduate of Auburn University at the time. He told her if she would go to Colorado with him, he would teach her how to ski. Off they went to the snowy slopes.

She had never seen a pair of skis, but she took to it like a goat to grass. She became an absolute daredevil on the slopes. Skip was still learning, and on many occasions while he was picking himself from a fall, she would go flying by laughing like crazy. Skip never went skiing again. Some things just don't work out.

I'll never forget the time Skip and Ron Jenkins were renting a house together in a quiet Decatur neighborhood. It was a lovely old house with a beautiful fireplace in the living room.

Ron is a wonderful cook, and they decided to invite some friends over for a chili supper. Ron would do all the cooking, of course, while Skip took on the job of building a nice fire in the living room fireplace.

When I arrived and Skip opened the front door, smoke hit me in the face.

"Skip," I suggested, "your house seems to be on fire."

"No," he replied. "I think there's something wrong with the fireplace."

I stepped inside and almost choked. There was a thick, thick layer of heavy smoke going from the ceiling to within about three feet of the floor.

"Is it supposed to do this?" he asked.

"Of course not!" I gasped. "Did you open the flue?"

"Open the what?"

While I was trying to get the flue open, the other guests were arriving. Skip answered the door on all fours, because you absolutely could not breathe when you were standing up. When I looked around, Skip had two couples crawling behind him into the living room.

The chili was good, but it's hard to enjoy

good cooking when you can't breathe.

In 1985, the Friendship Force invited Diane and me to the Soviet Union. When word got around that we were going, Skip called and asked if he could go, too. I told him I would check and see if they had room on the trip.

"See if I can take a woman," he asked.

I explained to him that the Friendship Force was an organization that represented high moral values and that I would find it awkward to ask if he could take a woman and share a room with her.

"Lud," he begged, "you know I hate to sleep alone even in America, and if I can't take somebody with me, I'm going to sleep in the same room with you and Diane."

I finally worked it out so he could take his friend along with him. It was a condition, however, that they have separate rooms.

Skip is helpless in the good old U.S. of A. In the Soviet Union, he was not to be believed.

In 1985 the Russians had not adopted Glasnost, and life was only a little better than it had been under Krushchev. They had a certain way of doing things, and all the rubles in the world wouldn't make them change it. When you check into a hotel, you are given a card. If it is a green card, you eat in the dining room with the green sign. If you are issued a red or blue card, you eat in the red or blue dining room. There are no exceptions. If there is a long line for the red dining room and no line for the green, and if you happen to have a red card, you simply wait in line. It doesn't make any sense, but it's life or death to them.

Skip, Diane, and I all had green cards. One early morning Diane and I were on our way to breakfast. As we walked past the blue dining room, we heard a man screaming at the very top of his lungs, "NYET! NYET! NYET!" Everyone in the hotel lobby ran to look into the blue dining room, where they saw Skip trying to pay a waiter for a cup of coffee he was carrying. Another one of their rules was that they would take no cash; all charges appeared on the hotel bill. So here was Skip, in the wrong dining room, helping himself to a cup of coffee and trying to pay a waiter with a dollar bill. The waiter was blue with rage, and Skip just kept on walking and poking the dollar at him. The waiter finally took the coffee and showed Skip through sign language that he wanted him out. Skip came up to us in the lobby looking totally baffled.

"Did you see that?" he asked. I told him I had. He said, "What in the hell was wrong with him?" I explained to him about the color of his card.

"But I offered him a dollar for one lousy cup of coffee." There was no understanding the Soviet Union, and if there had been, there was certainly no explaining it to Skip. It might have been his most frustrating moment in the Soviet Union, and he had many of them.

Once we were in a snack bar outside some palace or another. Skip had been suffering with an upset stomach, and while we were sitting there, Mother Nature called him very, very urgently. There was a public bathroom in the snack bar, but a public bathroom in the Soviet Union is generally a hole in the floor—and that's all.

Skip jumped up from the table and made a dash for the bathroom. He was gone for about thirty seconds before he reappeared in the doorway with panic in his voice and terror on his face.

"Lud," he cried out, "there's no toilet paper!"

Suddenly, I saw the light bulb come on over his head. He broke into a run around the snack bar, slowing down at every table to jerk the paper napkins out of the napkin holders. In about five minutes, he came out like nothing had happened. The Russians who were there must have thought they were in the presence of a madman.

It goes without saying that Skip did not understand the Soviets, and Lord knows the

Soviets did not understand him. If they had spoken English, I would have loved to interview the maids that cleaned his room in Moscow. There are no shower curtains, and if you want to keep the bathroom livable, you need to use a certain amount of care when you are taking your shower. I picked him up at his room one morning, and water was almost out in the hall. His room looked like a Muscovite Okeefenokee. I assumed from the volume of water that a pipe had burst, but when I asked what had happened, he blamed the deluge on not having a shower curtain. You'd think he would have compensated, but it was like he had taken an entire thirty-minute shower and *then* noticed that he didn't have a curtain.

During the short time we were there, Skip almost drowned in a bidet, bought two quarts of champagne from a Shiite Muslim who spoke no English, and almost missed the train from Leningrad to Moscow. The only man ever to confuse the Russians more than Skip was James Bond.

Skip, by his own admission, cannot operate anything that has a moving part. When I mentioned earlier that his VCR had been blinking twelve o'clock for four years, it was no exaggeration. In fact, he has recently co-authored a country-western song called "It's Always Midnight on My VCR." He says the remote control on his television is too complicated, and he therefore refuses to use it.

Skip recently paid four thousand dollars for a complete home entertainment unit. It is a work of art. In addition to the television, it has a CD player, a VCR, and a very fancy AM-FM radio. It is as useless to him as a one-handled wheelbarrow. It just sits there on a shelf looking pitiful. The only sign of life is the VCR, proclaiming to the world, twelve o'clock, twelve o'clock, twelve o'clock.

One night during baseball season when the Atlanta Braves were not on TV, Skip was unable to pick up the game on the AM radio of his four-grand entertainment center. He listened to the entire game sitting in his car. The people who sold him the center have sent a serviceman out twice, not to fix the equipment, but to explain to Skip how to turn it on.

It's not just electrical things or gadgets with moving parts that confound him. He spends about 250 nights a year in hotel rooms. If the shower has two knobs, one that says "H" and one that says "C," he does fine. If, however, it is any other type shower, he is either going to burn himself or suffer an icy blast. In an effort to make life easier for him, I suggested that when he could not figure out the shower, he should take a tub bath.

"If there is one thing on earth I can't stand," he declared, "it's washing my face in the same water I've been sitting in."

When he had a burglar alarm installed in his home, I knew the alarm company was going to earn every cent of its money. In the first few days after the system was installed, he accidently set if off seventeen times. Since he had no idea how to turn it off, the police came to his house every time. The company has been forced to impose a fifty-dollar charge for every false alarm.

His alarm system has what they call a panic button. It can be used to summon help should a bad guy get into the house. It looks like a garage door opener and can be carried around the house. One day Skip noticed it for the first time and said, "Wonder what this is?" He mashed the button, and all hell broke loose — sirens wailing and lights flashing. He knew at once what had happened, and he was so embarrassed that he went outside, got in his car, and drove away.

It almost goes without saying that Skip has trouble keeping his appointments and showing up for all his many engagements. It's not always his fault, but sometimes it is, and this occasional failing can put a real strain on a friendship.

Skip and Norman Arey have enjoyed a love-hate relationship for over twenty years.

Like all really close, masculine relationships, Skip and Norman love each other not because of their faults, but in spite of them. Their friendship has endured, I think, because they have so much in common. They are both gifted writers, they share a lifelong love of train travel, and both are tennis nuts.

The three of us were scheduled to do a local TV show some years ago. I don't recall exactly why we were appearing, but I think it was going to be a sports trivia show. We had met to make plans on five or six occasions. We were sure that we had a pretty good show put together, and since none of us had ever been on television, our enthusiasm was high and we were looking forward to doing the show.

On the day of the show, Norman called me and said, "You gotta do something about Skip."

"What's going on?" I asked.

"I just talked to him," explained Norman, "and he said he's not going to do the TV show tonight."

"Did he say why?"

"No," said Norman, clearly frustrated. "He just mumbled. You know how he mumbles when you try to pin him down."

I told Norman to calm down, that I would call Skipper and see if I could find out what the problem was. I got Skip on the phone and asked why he was not going to be with us on the tube.

"OhIdontknow," he mumbled. "Igotsomuchworktodo . . . Imjustcoveredup . . . IdontknowanythingaboutTV . . . Imtired . . . mumblemumblemumble."

"Skip," I pointed out, "we have been talking about this for a month. We have told everybody we would be there, and we just can't back out at this stage of the game."

"Mumblemumblemumble."

Finally, I said, "If you're not there, I'm going to come to your house, kill your dog, and break every bone in your body."

"I'll be there."

"Good! Now why did you call Norman and get him so upset?"

"Well," he said, "Norman didn't explain it to me like you did."

Once, a couple of years ago, Norman called me to fuss about Skip. In the course of the conversation, he said, "Lud, I know how close you and Skip are, and I hate to say it, but Skip has not handled success well."

"Don't forget, Norman," I reminded him, "Skip didn't handle failure well either."

Just a
Bowl of
Butterbeans

One of the things I love best about Skip Grizzard is that he is Southern to the marrow and proud of it. He also has certain Southern quirks, one of the funniest of which is his attitude toward food.

Skip is forty-five years old and, by his own admission, has never had a healthy meal in his life. He has been married and divorced three times. He has been engaged to all the eligible women in the seven southeastern states and certain parts of Florida. In his forty-five years, he has held over twenty jobs, traveled all over the world, and judged a goat milk-off in Abbyville, Louisiana. The only consistent thing in his life seems to be the Waffle House. It is his favorite restaurant in the whole world. He seems to feel a oneness with all Waffle House employees. He proudly proclaims that they are the only people in the world who can fix eggs "over medium well." I never heard of eggs "over medium well," but he is convinced that that is the only way Christian people should eat eggs.

He was having breakfast one morning at the Marriott Hotel in New Orleans. The waiter was named Keith. Skip ordered bacon, grits, and two eggs "over medium well." Keith said nothing, but his eyebrows went up about two inches. He returned with the breakfast. Skip poked into the yellow part of his egg and said in a disgusted tone,

"These eggs are not over medium well. They are over, by God, raw!"

Keith straightened his little black bow tie and said, "I will tell the chef, sir."

He removed Skip's breakfast and returned to the kitchen. When he came back a few minutes later, Skip took one look and said, "I wish to hell I was at the Waffle House. These eggs are not over medium well."

"Pardon me, sir," harrumphed Keith, "but could you describe exactly what 'over medium well' means."

Skip took a deep breath and said, " 'Over medium well' means that the yellow is not running toward the edge of the plate. The yellow is *crawling* toward the edge of the plate."

"Crawling, sir?" asked Keith.

"You got it," confirmed Skip.

He took the plate and disappeared into the kitchen for the third time. When he returned, he said, "I hope these will be satisfactory, sir."

"The eggs are perfect," said Skip, "but everything else is cold."

It was at this point that Keith had what can only be described as a complete emotional breakdown. He buried his face in a napkin and started to cry. He ran from the table sobbing uncontrollably. Skip dipped his cold toast into his over medium well eggs and, with a puzzled look on his face, asked, "Reckon what's wrong with old Keith?"

Keith is only one in a long line of servers whose emotional well-being has been put in jeopardy by Skip.

Skip decided early on that grits were some kind of health food. As a result, he adds either bacon or sausage grease, a large dob of cowbutter, and loads of black pepper. Any healthful properties belonging to grits are more than made up for with these additions. He calls his concoction "Grits Grizzard," a dish that has been now outlawed by the health departments in three states.

Whenever possible, Skip tries to order only white food for breakfast. He orders his now-famous eggs over medium well, grits, and biscuits with sawmill gravy poured over them. It is entirely possible that one could go snow blind eating breakfast with Skip.

He thinks the four basic food groups are the Waffle House, Harold's, the Varsity, and Sweat's Barbecue.

Once, while traveling in Europe, he was offered some squid. He declined, saying that he had once seen the movie *20,000 Leagues Under the Sea* and he would not eat anything Kirk Douglas could not kill.

Skip likes all Southern-style food. As a matter of fact, that is the only style of food he really loves. Once, while driving to the Gator Bowl in Jacksonville, we decided that we wanted a real Southern gourmet meal. We had been staying at Hilton Head Island for a week preceding the game, and while Hilton Head is in South Carolina and in the Deep South, the food in all the restaurants there is decidedly yankee.

We were going south on I-95 and stopped at a place called Kitty's Kountry Kitchen. I learned at my mother's knee that you should never eat in a place where the owner spells "country" with a "k." Common sense will tell you that anybody who can't spell "country" sure as heck can't read a cookbook. We looked at the menu and noticed that the first item said simply, "Chicken." The waiter was an Oriental gentleman with a name tag that read, "Earl."

"How is the chicken prepared?" asked Skip.

"It is smothered, sir," replied Earl.

"I don't care how you killed it," Skip declared. "What I want to know is, do you have any fried chicken?"

"Fried chicken is not good for you," Earl answered. "Too much grease."

"Earl," said Skip with a frown, "are you here to wait on tables or practice medicine?"

A quick check of the menu showed that there was nothing mashed, fried, or starchy. So we left, unfed. We walked out into the

parking lot, by this time starving to death.
Across the street from Kitty's Kountry
Kitchen was an old clapboard store. The
hand-lettered sign out front said, "Walt's
Texaco/Grocery Store/Notary."

Skip lit up like a carnival midway.
"Come on," he said. "We're going to have a
real Southern meal."

We walked across the road. There were
double screen doors that said, "Colonial
Bread is Good Bread," in bright yellow and
orange letters. There was a fist-sized ball of
cotton fastened to the top of the screen. The
inside of the store was dark even though the
lights were on.

"Come in the house," said the old man
behind the counter as we pulled open the
screen door.

"How ya doin'?" we asked.

"Never been better and had less," he
answered. "Can I hep ya?"

"We're going to have us a little dinner,"
Skip said.

"You pick it out, and I'll ring her up,"
said Walt.

Skip was absolutely beaming as we
walked around the old store shopping. There
was a bright red drink box against the wall.
The yellow writing on it said, "Royal Crown
Cola . . . Best by Taste Test." We pulled two
six-and-a-half-ounce Cokes out of the freezing cold, murky water. We then bought a box

of soda crackers and a loaf of white bread. We continued to wander around and found the sardines, two Moon Pies, a box of Fig Newtons, and some pork and beans. Skip hollered to Walt at the front of the store, "You got any baloney?"

"Was Eleanor Roosevelt ugly?" Walt hollered back. "You know I got baloney."

He escorted us back to the meat counter, where we ordered six slices of baloney. He cut them off with a knife.

"Speck you gonna need some cheese, ain't ya?" he asked.

"We need about a hunk or a hunk and a half of cheese," Skip answered.

We bought paper plates, plastic spoons, and a 49-cent can opener. While we were paying Walt, I noticed two signs on the wall behind the old brass cash register. One said, "Jesus loves you." The sign directly below it read, "Absolutely no credit."

Walt bade us farewell by saying, "Y'all hurry back."

We pulled the car under the shade of a giant live oak tree and spread our South Georgia luau on the hood of the car. I don't know if it was my hunger or my Southern roots, but it was probably one of my top two or three all-time memorable meals.

When we had finished our last Fig Newton, we sat down in the grass to finish our Coke and savor the moment.